# Leadership

## Volume 6B of the series

### *Discovering Infinity*

A science discovery series
by Rolf A. F. Witzsche

Published by Cygni Communications Ltd.
North Vancouver, BC, Canada
(http://books.rolf-witzsche.com)

Cover image by Corel Corp

**Is our goal victory,
or to raise the standard of achievement?**

In sports the goal is victory, though the standard may be raised. In the larger sphere of life the goal of leadership is to establish new standards for achievement that uplifts an entire nation, civilization, even mankind as a whole. In that case, victories may result along the way as in the case of Russia's victory over Napoleon. When Russia was hopelessly challenged a new standard had been set by Germany's poet Friedrich Schiller who was already dead at the time, by whose higher standard of humanity Russia's victory was won. That's an example of leadership. - Research by Rolf Witzsche based on the work of Mary Baker Eddy and Lyndon H. LaRouche Jr..

This book is Volume 6B, of the research series, *Discovering Infinity*.

The research series, *Discovering Infinity*, was originally created over the span of two decades, beginning in the late 1980s, and was updated periodically. The series is structured as two sets of three volumes, with each set corresponding to the three-step sequence of Hell, Purgatory, and Paradise that we find in the poetic trilogy the Divine Comedy by Dante Alighierie created in the early 1300s. The first set of three volumes of the series Discovering Infinity represents the view of Dante's "pilgrim," while the second set represents the view of his "guide." In some cases a volume of this series is made up of several distinct books. For more details, see the appendix: About the research series, Discovering Infinity.

In parallel with the research series *Discovering Infinity* a series of twelve novels with the summary title, The lodging for the Rose, was created. The platform of the novel was deemed necessary for this different venue of exploration since the real dimension of love tends to become lost on any kind of theoretical platform, rather than be born out as a light to uplift civilization from the grassroots level up. The individual titles of the series of novels are shown in the appendix: More works by the author. The series *The Lodging for the Rose* has two individual novels leading into it as a kind of preface that is gently opening the portal to the Principle of Universal Love, which is the main theme of the series of twelve novels, *The Lodging for the Rose*. The Principle of Universal Love is the thread that ties both series together.

# Contents

# Leadership

How does one define spirituality in the modern world? The dictionary definitions vary and cover a broad range of concepts including those related to extracorporeal existence, intellectual endowments, moral feelings, expressions of the soul, or church related devotion or zeal. In other words, the dictionary can't define what spirituality is, but it brings together a multitude of diverse perceptions. If one considers this diversity, one might conclude that spirituality is a subject that no one can really understand. But this is not so. To the contrary, spirituality is native to every human being. Almost everyone is aware of it, and benefits from it. Herein lies its proof. But what, specifically, is it? How can one define it?

Two historic pioneers come to mind who can speak on the subject with authority by virtue of their proven spirituality that became manifest in spiritual processes of healing. One such pioneer and spiritual authority was Christ Jesus. The man appeared at the pinnacle of a spiritual renaissance that began with Homer in Greece and included such names in its chain of development as Solon, Socrates, Plato. The man also had a strong background in Hebrew culture with a history centered on a type of monotheism in which spiritual healing had played a significant role. Christ Jesus is renowned for his outstanding spiritual healing work; but did he say anything specific that defines the nature of spirituality itself?

One must assume that he said a great deal on the subject, although the term didn't exist in those days. His most direct comment on spirituality may be the one found in the answer to a query by a woman who evidently asked herself a similar question; " Our fathers worshipped in this mountain;" she said, "and ye say, that in Jerusalem is the place where men ought to worship."

The Bible reports:
21 Jesus saith unto her, Woman, believe me, the hour cometh, when ye shall neither in this mountain, nor yet at Jerusalem, worship the Father.
24 God is a Spirit: and they that worship him must worship him in spirit and in truth.
John 4

The problem with this type of definition for spirituality is, that it is not one that one can "sink one's teeth in," so to speak. However, there exists another definition that fulfills this criteria better. He had counseled the people at one point:

23 ...if thou bring thy gift to the altar, and there rememberest that thy brother hath ought against thee;
24 Leave there thy gift before the altar, and go thy way; first be reconciled to thy brother, and then come and offer thy gift.
Matthew 5

The problem that emerges in this case, is, that the essence of the statement is covered by common morality and is rarely perceived as a specific aspect of spirituality. Thus, one needs to search further for a clearer example. Such a one was recorded by the apostle Luke:

25 ... behold, a certain lawyer stood up, and tempted him, saying, Master, what shall I do to inherit eternal life?
26 He said unto him, What is written in the law? how readest thou?
27 And he answering said, Thou shalt love the Lord thy God with all thy heart, and with all thy soul, and with all thy strength, and with all thy mind; and thy neighbour as thyself.
28 And he said unto him, Thou hast answered right: this do, and thou shalt live.
29 But he, willing to justify himself, said unto Jesus, And who is my neighbour?
30 And Jesus answering said, A certain man went down from Jerusalem to Jericho, and fell among thieves, which stripped him of his raiment, and wounded him, and departed, leaving him half dead.
31 And by chance there came down a certain priest that way: and when he saw him, he passed by on the other side.
32 And likewise a Levite, when he was at the place, came and looked on him, and passed by on the other side.
33 But a certain Samaritan, as he journeyed, came where he was: and

when he saw him, he had compassion
on him,
34 And went to him, and bound up
his wounds, pouring in oil and
wine, and set him on his own beast,
and brought him to an inn, and took
care of him.
35 And on the morrow when he
departed, he took out two pence,
and gave them to the host, and said
unto him, Take care of him; and
whatsoever thou spendest more, when
I come again, I will repay thee.
Luke 10

Here, Christ Jesus spoke of compassion, of pouring in "oil" and "wine," and of putting the man on his own beast. Isn't that what Christ Jesus had done himself, in all aspects of healing. The Scriptures say about his healing work that he acted with "compassion," and that he thereby, literally, put the patient on "his own beast," his own standard. In other words, he raised the man up unto the same platform of worth where he found his own identity as a man. He could not do otherwise. Honesty to the truth required this. The spirituality that had pervaded his consciousness with fundamental truths could never allow him to deny what he understood of the nature of man in its reflection of the image of God. This is, evidently, what Christ Jesus saw reflected in the First Commandment, or the great commandment of the law.

In the above example, we have a measure of spirituality defined that severely challenges the modern convention, but Christ Jesus' comment was: "This do, and thou shalt live."*1

This comment to the lawyer who had desired to know the essence of life, is highly significant, because his answer, "This do, and thou shalt live," was not just an empty saying. If one probes beneath the surface it becomes apparent that questions centered on spirituality invariably involve life and death issues. The question, therefore, must be explored to the fullest.

"This do, and ye shall live," said Christ Jesus. Why did he say this? Was he right in saying this? The answer must be, yes. One must even ask, can anything be healed on any other basis?

Before answering, let us explore what lies behind these questions. Here, an incident comes to mind that closely echoes Christ Jesus' parable of the Samaritan. A man had addressed an audience of community leaders, among which businessmen and obviously knowledgeable financial experts. The presentation was in part centered on the role that the financier George Soros had played in unleashing the financial and economic chaos in Asia, how his manipulations of national currencies, for profit, had destroyed currency values and stock market values throughout the entire region. As commander of the Quantum Fund, an off-shore investment fund that contains more play-money then the operational budget funds of many a nation, he has the power to break the back of any nation at will. His primary target, of course are those nations where strong economic activity had created considerable wealth for the nation as a whole, that thereby could be looted. One of the audience, then, stood up in defense of George Soros, and said that it was Soros right to exploit the weakness of those who had failed to protect themselves, adding: "He merely exploited an opportunity..."

The speaker replied, by saying: "So you believe it is anyone's right to take an axe, break down a neighbor's door, and steal everything the neighbor has, or even wait until the neighbor's front door might have been left unlocked, and then do the stealing."

The speaker didn't go further than this. He might have pointed out that the entire world-financial market operates on this platform. In a world where the physical economies are contracting, the enormous profiteering that is going on in these markets amounts to nothing less then theft. The defenders of the market, point out that the markets operate fundamentally as zero sum game, by which the total wealth of society is not affected. In other words, there are as many winners as there are losers. The same, of course, can also be said about a person stealing from a neighbor. The priest in Jesus' parable represents the man who believes in the zero sum game and walks by. Except, this is not the type of platform on which nations are built. The zero sum platform is a platform of decay. The man who was robbed, injured, and left to die, no longer produces any wealth for society. In other words, the zero sum game is a lie. The current economic disintegration of the western world reflects this lie.

Was the Samaritan "a bleeding heart socialist," then, as some might insist that he was? One must say that he wasn't. In as much as a society cannot profit by stealing from each other, but destroys itself in the process, it cannot profit by giving its wealth away to anyone who asks for it, or because of an unproductive life, needs it. Nor is this what the Samaritan did. The Samaritan is illustrated to have used his riches to uplift the injured man to the point that he could be a productive member of society again. He is illustrated as one who didn't see the injured man as a liability, but as a valuable asset to society that needs to be protected at all cost. Christ Jesus perceived man as the son of God. This perception was also the foundation of the Renaissance. A society that does any less, cannot stand.

Its civilization disintegrates with a corresponding loss of life. Nor can a Christian healer who fails to operate **from** this tall platform, achieve anything of substance.

Was Christ Jesus correct, then, when he added this comment to the parable: "This do, and ye shall live?"

Before trying to answer this question, let us explore another question first. Can Christ Jesus' type of spirituality still be regarded as a valid factor as we face the third millennium A.D.?

Indeed, one should ask this question. The turn of the millennium, which the world will celebrate in a few years, is significant only in that it is referenced to the birth of that man who gave humanity a tall spiritual perception of itself. What he did was so momentous, that it had caused a portion of humanity to assume the name Christianity. It is no secret that Christ Jesus had defined spirituality by a broad range of manifestations that together projected a brighter image of mankind than any other that had ever been presented on this planet, so much so that humanity saw in it the beginning of a new era. Consequently, mankind had chosen to measure all its future ages against this point of reference. But is this reference justified? Should mankind not have chosen a different point of reference?

Evidence suggests that no better reference point could have been chosen. The Christ idea that this man has exemplified, if one puts all the religious underpinning aside, stands as a foundation on which all progressive aspects of mankind's civilization rest. Every progressive period in history has had at its root the scientific spiritual ideology that this man has established, or a fundamentally similar ideology. The Golden Renaissance, for instance, that began in the 15th century, one and a half millennia after the initial Christ-era, was solidly built on the Christ idea that Jesus had pioneered which presents man as reflecting the image of God.

This tall idea was born out in Jesus' days in the form of a profound capability to achieve a physical deliverance from diseases and death. In the days of the Renaissance (renewal), the rediscovery of the original Christ idea had ushered in an age of social, scientific, technological, and cultural progress that has had no equal in any age since, right to the present. Even now, mankind still benefits from the structures created in this period. The institution of the nation state is one of these. It was first pioneered in France, under Louis XI (1462), and later had its most advanced manifest in the organization of the sovereign nation-state of the United States of America (1776) by which that nation became the freest and most prosperous nation on earth until its principles were abandoned.

All this identifies in its own way the yardstick that mankind has chosen to measure its history, and hopefully itself. This yardstick, naturally, is a purely spiritual one.

The core element of Christ Jesus' legacy was the spiritual identity that he had illustrated and demonstrated, which had resurfaced during the Renaissance and had set the course for a renewal of mankind's self-development.

Christ Jesus had been a pioneer, working at the leading edge of scientific enquiry, exploring spiritual realities that had never been discovered before. This pioneering principle was brought out again during the Renaissance in terms of scientific discoveries and technological and cultural advances, the likes of which have never been seen before on the planet.

The other historic pioneer whose spirituality was manifest in a widely demonstrated ability for healing, on a Christ-like foundation, was Mary Baker Eddy. While her written works fill volumes, she rarely focuses on Christ Jesus' spirituality in such detail as she does in the following text. She wrote:

---

"It is related in the seventh chapter of Luke's Gospel that Jesus was once the honored guest of a certain Pharisee, by name Simon, though he was quite unlike Simon the disciple. While they were at meat, an unusual incident occurred, as if to interrupt the scene of Oriental festivity. A "strange woman" came in. Heedless of the fact that she was debarred from such a place and such society, especially under the stern rules of rabbinical law, as positively as if she were a Hindoo pariah intruding upon the household of a high-caste Brahman, this woman (Mary Magdalene, as she has since been called) approached Jesus. Why did he thus summarize her debt to divine Love? Had she repented and reformed, and did his insight detect this unspoken moral uprising? She bathed his feet with her tears before she anointed them with the oil. In the absence of other proofs, was her grief sufficient evidence to warrant the expectation of her repentance, reformation, and growth in wisdom? Certainly there was encouragement in the mere fact that she was showing her affection for a man of undoubted goodness and purity, who has since been rightfully regarded as the best man that ever trod this planet. Her reverence was unfeigned, and it was manifested towards one who was soon, though they knew it not, to lay down his mortal existence in behalf of all sinners, that through his word and works they might be redeemed from sensuality and sin."

"Which was the higher tribute to such ineffable affection, the hospitality of the Pharisee or the contrition of the Magdalen? This query Jesus answered by rebuking self-righteousness and declaring the absolution of the penitent. He even said that this poor woman had done what his rich entertainer had neglected to do, - wash and anoint his guest's feet, a special sign of Oriental courtesy."

"Here is suggested a solemn question, a question indicated by one of the needs of this age. Do Christian Scientists seek Truth as Simon sought the Savior, through material conservatism and for personal homage? Jesus told Simon that such seekers as he gave small reward in return for the spiritual purgation which came through the Messiah. If Christian Scientists are like Simon, then it must be said of them also that they love little."

---

She Adds:

---

"If the Scientist reaches his patient through divine Love, the healing work will be accomplished at one visit, and the disease will vanish into its native nothingness like dew before the morning sunshine. If the Scientist has enough Christly affection to win his own pardon, and such commendation as the Magdalen gained from Jesus, then he is Christian enough to practice scientifically and deal with his patients compassionately; and the result will correspond with the spiritual intent."*2

---

Here, another question emerges. What kind of pioneer stands at the leading edge, today? Who stands at the portal to infinity? What kind of a pioneer does one look for? Does one look for another Moses, or Plato, or Christ Jesus, or Mary Baker Eddy? No! Why should one? Whatever these people have achieved, remains. The need it to go forward. The need is to expand the horizon of healing. Today, the whole of humanity is in greater danger than it ever was. This means that the healing process must match the dynamics of this greater danger. The principles of the healing process must logically remain the same, but the application must be more spiritual and universal than ever before.

One might hear some protests here. "The world has changed," people say. Indeed it has. Still, in spite of the modern advances, the yardstick that mankind has chosen to measure itself with, remains a spiritual one. It comes to light in the form of discoveries that reveal a higher power in the unfolding focus on Mind, Principle, Truth, Life, Love, etc.. This higher power that comes to light in the above domains has been referred to in many cultures as God.

Sure enough, these definitive terms for the recognized higher power, or God, are all modern terms. But in the historic sense, these terms represents a dimension that has elevated the image of man to divine heights, not through mythologies, but through accomplishments. This higher dimension has opened the door to unprecedented freedoms. No one before and after Christ Jesus has demonstrated mankind's dominion over limitations to a greater degree than was demonstrated during the historic period when Christ Jesus healed the sick, fed the multitudes, walked on the water, and raised the dead.

Still, over the ages the human genius has achieved far more than this. Today's modern technologies feed infinitely greater multitudes of people than those that Christ Jesus had once fed in the dessert of Judea. While mankind has not yet learned to walk on the waters, it has demonstrated its ability to walk on the moon. Scientifically, and spiritually, mankind has raised the 'dead' as Jesus did, but on a universal plain, by means of dramatic increases in the life expectancy of every person on the planet, compared to that which prevailed 2000 years ago. These larger achievements have all been possible through principled mind action.

In a very real sense, the parameters for spirituality that have been established by Christ Jesus, are still valid. But how would one expect to find them exemplified?

Christ Jesus, himself, once commented on this question as to how the advance guard of progress is to be measured. John the Baptist had sent messengers to Christ Jesus inquiring of him, "Art thou he that should come, or do we look for another?" There was no direct answer provided by Christ Jesus except to tell the messengers:

> Go and shew John again those
> things which ye do hear and see:
> 5 The blind receive their sight,
> and the lame walk, the lepers are
> cleansed, and the deaf hear, the
> dead are raised up, and the poor
> have the gospel preached to them.
> 6 And blessed is he, whosoever
> shall not be offended in me.
> Matthew 11

Mary Baker Eddy applied the same type of yardstick to answer the critics who disagreed with her reasoning. While she had had made great strides forward, the shallow perception in public thinking was insufficient to break the axioms that hold the human spirit shackled to so many limits - limits that she, the pioneer, could see beyond.

Mary Baker Eddy writes:"I was once called to visit a sick man to whom the regular physicians had given three doses of Croton oil, and then had left him to die. Upon my arrival I found him barely alive, and in terrible agony. In one hour he was well, and the next day he attended to his business. I removed the stoppage, healed him of enteritis, and neutralized the bad effects of the poisonous oil. His physicians had failed even to move his bowels, - though the wonder was, with the means used in their effort to accomplish this result, that they had not quite killed him. According to their diagnosis, the exciting cause of the inflammation and stoppage was - eating smoked herring. The man is living yet; and I will send his address to any one who may wish to apply to him for information about his case."

Mary Baker Eddy explains, "Divine metaphysics is that which treats of the existence of God, His essence, relations, and attributes. A sneer at metaphysics is a scoff at Deity; at His goodness, mercy, and might. - Christian Science is the unfolding of true metaphysics; that is, of Mind, or God, and His attributes. Science rests on Principle and demonstration. The Principle of Christian Science is divine. Its rule is, that man shall utilize the divine power. In Genesis i. 26, we read: "Let us make man in our image, after our likeness: and let them have dominion over the fish of the sea, and over the fowl of the air.""*3

Mary Baker Eddy presents in the above text a remarkable additional parameter that defines spirituality, as she draws together into an interlocking unity the concepts of "goodness, mercy, and might."

Now, let us bring these three qualities into context with the parable of the Samaritan, presented earlier. The Samaritan has never been seen as a mighty man, has he? But in real terms, he was. By his actions he established the social environment that he preferred to live in, an environment in which the truth was respected, in which the dignity of the human being counted for something. The priest and the Levite might have desired to raise the spiritual status of the society, but the priesthood had accomplished little in this line as it was working outside the parameters of spirituality where truth is the center for motives and action.

The priest was impotent in responding to the spiritual fact. His spirituality was theoretical. It consisted of a front of words with no depth or substance. The priest had no option open to him, but to walk by.

Not so the Samaritan. What that man encountered by the wayside violated what he understood about the value and dignity of man. On the strength of this spiritual perception, he acted and corrected the scene, thereby protecting the environment of truth that he cherished. It was therefore with evident ease that he turned a most ugly situation into a beautiful manifest of the nature of man. What he did, evidently was of greater power to raise the status of the society in which he lived, himself, than anything the priests or Levite had ever achieved. He was a mighty man, indeed, one who had changed and uplifted society.

However, was Christ Jesus justified in suggesting that this type of spirituality is essential to maintaining life?

It appears that he was justified in suggesting this. The response by the priest, and by the Samaritan, in the parable, stand in contrast to each other. This contrast manifests the deeper contrast that is apparent between a social platform built on spirituality, and that which is devoid of spirituality.

Let's examine what a social platform looks like that is devoid of spirituality. One finds many examples among today's "me" generation where the focus doesn't extend an inch beyond a person's skin and bank account. It doesn't matter to such a person that many people are finding themselves subjected to poverty, homelessness, and life-threatening deprivations, brought about by policies from which the 'successful' profit. A person with such a focus is more concerned about being able to import cheap slave labor products produced in foreign nations, than in building a healthy social environment with a productive industrial base that raises the riches of the entire society. In real terms, no one can derive profit from any process that does not elevate the whole of society and enrich it. It cannot be done. We all live in the world that we create. No one lives apart from it.

Those who live for personal profit, invariably are thieves and murderers, and invariably walk by the human equation, on the other side as it were.

Christ Jesus named only two examples of those who walk by on the other side. In today's world one finds countless more. Some don't need to be named. And, then, there are those who walk by unintentionally. These are they who were educated to either close their eyes and minds to the reality that surrounds them, or who regard black as white because of what they are told in the newspapers to be true.

People who "walk by," and disregard the human need for uplifting the whole of society, do injure themselves by their noninvolvement or lack of response to the principles involved. This is true, because, if there is a void of spirituality manifest, this void necessarily manifests itself as fascism. The none-involved, without knowing it, become tools for fascism, and in the end fall pray to fascism.

The above is a strong statement, but it is supported by history. The question may be asked how was it possible for the spiritually most advanced culture, the Greek Classical culture, to be so deeply engulfed by the Roman terror that the nation's population, itself, became reduced by 87% over the space of the Roman period. The answer is, that this regression has a lot to do with walking by on the other side, which amounts to a support of the failing system. Aristotle had a lot to do with this turn-around who argued for the right to accumulate wealth by clever means of stealing. His name became synonymous with the classes of society who maintain this right to the present day, called the Aristocracy. It is not by accident, either, that Aristotle's theory of natural slavery, in which the master races by virtue of a presumed 'higher' intellect have assumed the right to enslave 'lesser' human beings, is reflected in the Aristocracy's history as the slave trader of the world.

This still happens to the very day, although the form has slightly changed. Black slavery on plantations has given way to 'civil' slavery in maliquadori around the world, and to child slavery that is all by itself 100 larger than the African slavery ever was. The products of 250 million children, that are now enslaved in the poor nations around the globe, together with countless adults working in sweat shops, food the rich nations under global free trade, which, because of their cheap price, displace the products of the civil work forces to the point that entire industries disintegrate. Today, most of humanity actively participates in the crime that consumes the new generation. Most people readily purchase the slavery products that save them a penny. What a profit is being wrought here! The people who run this world-trade in human slavery for their own profit, as an operation for looting, still call themselves the Aristocracy.

The Greek Classical culture experienced a sharp turn-around after Aristotle. Aristotle countered the spiritual unfolding that Plato had represented. A new development began that Aristotle represented, that had its ultimate reflection in the political structure of the Roman Empire. The Aristotealian shift was further enhanced with the concentration of financial riches that were enabled with the advanced economic status of Greece as the most culturally and technologically advanced nation of that period. However, the new riches were not equally shared, as they were gauged from speculative trade rather than being the result of universal development. The 'success' that some had in extracting riches from others through trade was deemed a virtue under Aristotle's ideology. Let the 'successful' steal as they will, and let the victims (the unsuccessful) perish as they must for their natural weakness. This became an unspoken motto. Later, this motto became mirrored in the ideology of Rome.

Under this motto no one cared about the victims who were slaughtered in the many arenas. The entire gladiatorial entertainment scene was built on slaughtering the 'unsuccessful.' This motto that was pioneered by Aristotle had the effect to shut out spirituality, and this quite effectively so.

The countless thousands who observed the slaughtering of the 'unsuccessful' during the festivals of Rome, which became evermore numerous, both in Rome itself and in Roman capitals of occupation, cheered as the victims were put to death by the victors in the games, or by wild animals let loose against people tied defenseless to wooden stakes. As this fascism escalated, and the demand for victims increased, many a person who cheered before wound up sooner or later on the floor of the arena. The atmosphere that this disrespect for the human being had created, represents an extreme case of walking by on the other side, which quickly became an atmosphere of doom. By its escalating fascism that any void of spirituality brings about, the Roman society had become literally unfit to survive.

That the wholesale murdering in Rome was not an isolated case, is evident by the economic devastation that is currently sweeping the world. When the IMF began quietly to raise its ugly head against the poor nations in tropical regions, demanding austerity upon austerity, the 'rich' world closed its eyes and pretended not to see the pain and the dying. The resulting defeat of its spiritual conscience soon enabled the same austerity to be imposed on its own shores. This escalation has now reached a point at which austerity has become a global phenomenon that is murdering an estimated 100 million people each year. And the game still escalates.

The fact becomes evermore pronounced, that, whenever one finds a lack of spirituality, one finds a tendency towards fascism, because without spirituality one is confined onto a domain of conflicts with having the resources to confront the conflicts with corrective measures. On the other hand, someone with a highly developed spirituality cannot help to embrace in his efforts to uplift the human scene, the whole of humanity. In Truth, humanity is one, and the whole of humanity is supported by the same principle. One cannot mock these by drawing dividing lines across humanity. To do so, would imply that one doesn't know anything about them. One has no choice, but to embrace all humanity. This, however, ties spirituality to politics.

The American statesman and economist, Lyndon LaRouche, has often been criticized for being involved in the international arena. "Are there not enough problems at home to correct?" some people say. It should be noted that Franklin Delanor Roosevelt has likewise been severely criticized by Churchill for his determination to halt colonialism around the world, and to cause global economic development that would have given some meaning to the world's struggle against Hitler's fascism.

The fact is, F. D. Roosevelt and Churchill had operated precisely from the two diverse platforms that Christ Jesus so vividly illustrated with the parable of the Samaritan. According to the platform that Christ Jesus has outlined, neither F. D. Roosevelt nor Lyndon LaRouche could see an option open not to get involved. Whoever understands the infinite range of the human intellect, and its power for discovery and self-development towards a boundless horizon, cannot walk idly by or make a detour around humanity which lies injured by fascism, or the effects of their own fascism arising from insanity. This option does not exist for anyone who is concerned about truth and justice. Furthermore, concern for truth and justice is the natural manifest of spirituality. Truth and justice are not found on any other platform.

Whoever speaks of spirituality, as literally every religious organization on the planet does, but speaks and acts contemptuously about humanity or shows no concern about advancing truth and justice, is far from dealing with spirituality at all. Such persons are involved in mythology and self-delusion. Christ Jesus made this quite clear in the parable of the Samaritan. Love for humanity in the proof of the pudding, as it were, which necessarily involves a concern for truth and justice. Christ Jesus pointed out strongly that nothing less will do. "This do, and thou shalt live!"*4

Lyndon LaRouche makes no speeches about spirituality, but he does talk about all the various aspects that are the outcome of a highly developed spirituality. He urges governments to adopt policies of economic justice, policies that develop the human potential, that develop industries, food, housing, efficient transportation, new energy systems, and whatever else is essential to raise civilization to a higher level. He urges the adoption of policies that protect the rights of humanity, the rights of human beings to life, liberty, and the pursuit of happiness, rather then the rights of property, or the self-assumed rights of a tiny minority who demands to be allowed to steal from humanity whatever they choose to steal for their wealthy and opulent living.

Lyndon LaRouche teaches spirituality by focusing on the aspects that are the outcome of it. He focuses on art, science, music, poetry, drama, as well as on discoveries of fundamental principles and the technologies that are developed from the discoveries. His focus is on developing the character of individuals in order to lay a foundation in understanding upon which policies can be created that elevate civilization.

It is very well possible that spirituality is more truly and intensely promoted by this single man, than by all the preachers in all the churches combined. The proof on which this statement is based is the glaring disinterest that one finds among society to protect itself against those who loot away its living, who destroy its industries upon which its living depends, who destroy the currencies and financial systems that support the physical economies that provide food, clothing, housing, and the multitude of other aspect that define our modern civilization. The sad fact is, that Lyndon LaRouche stands presently alone in the field of protecting humanity against the impending catastrophe of a global financial disintegration.

He is a pioneer and a leader in a world of deaf ears and blinded eyes. If one considers the countless churches that operate around the world, there should be thousands of people like him who carry the torch for humanity. But where are they? They are not to be found. His leadership stands in isolation in a world that has closed its eyes to reality. And yet, his efforts are felt around the world. His policy proposals are discussed in China, Russia, Malaysia, even while he is laughed at at home.

Where then are the would be leaders who should have pushed for policies to reign in the kind of massive financial speculation that can destroy the currencies of entire nations, and has done so many times over. Lyndon LaRouche once called for policies to impose a 0.1% tax on financial speculation in order to protect humanity. But society was unresponsive. The price for this lack of response is paid in human lives lost as once prosperous nations like South Korea, Indonesia, Malaysia, saw their currencies devalued by as much as 90%, in some cases, which destroyed their economies and financial sectors and opened the nation to more intense looting by the international oligarchy.

The above calamity could not have happened if society as a whole had developed the kind of spirituality that Lyndon LaRouche is promoting on the full front of his organization by means of its focus on all the numerous aspects that raise the status of civilization. This is how patriots are created. But still his leadership stands largely in isolation. A massive drive was launched to encourage President Clinton to accept his leadership as his economics advisor, but this availed little since the President, himself, was confined to the domain of conflicts to which real leadership appears disgustingly revolutionary. Indeed, it would have opened the doors of the self-made confinement as it would have caused confrontations that would have resolved many of the paradoxes that hand over humanity today. But neither can Lyndon LaRouche back off.

Those who perceive the potential and the dignity of the human being, cannot at the same time trample upon it, or watch it being trampled upon by fascist boots. The only option that such people see before them, is to raise up humanity to the realization of its potential. So far, Lyndon LaRouche and his organization stand alone in promoting the platform of universal development for the full realization of mankind's potential while much of the world stands aside in silence, even though the whole world would profit immensely if his development proposals were accepted. Except, he is not alone in being rejected in this manner.

There were a few others in history who had promoted the same or similar option. The most notable of these were the Philadelphia Interests centered around Henry Carey in the USA (in the 1800s) who had envisioned to engage the combined economic potential of Germany and America to develop Russia and Asia to the same level of productive potential that the two leading industrial nations, themselves had enjoyed. This would have corresponded in principle to the action that Christ Jesus illustrated in the parable of the Samaritan who had raised the man up from his injuries. History, of course, records that this did not happen. Instead, British diplomacy set the nations as war with each other. War has always been the Empire's favorite tool to prevent the development of humanity.

Instead of the world standing up for itself, and aiding the development of Asia that would have sparked the development of the whole world, the world stood aside and allowed the British Empire launch two devastating dope wars against China that destroyed the potential of this nation, and impose irrational nationalist ideologies in Europe that set the nations of Europe at each other's throat for their eventual self-destruction. More then 30 million people lost their life as a consequence of the world's apathy in protecting itself, and many times more in one considers the consequences of the world-wide economic development that did not happen. This massive tragedy would not have happened had the principle been understood that Christ Jesus illustrated in the parable. Was Christ Jesus justified, therefore, in saying: "This do, and thou shalt live?"

The same devastating disinterest was encountered in the next century, too, a few years after the dust had settled from the fallout of World War I. Dr. Sun Yat-sen of China suggested virtually the same thing the Philadelphia interests around Henry Carey had suggested. Dr. Sun Yat-sen proposed that the industrial potential of the world that had supplied the theatres of war in Europe, should be employed to its fullest capacity for the development of China, from which, again, the whole world would have benefitted. This, again, would have been in accord with the principle that Christ Jesus has illustrated in the parable of the Samaritan. Dr. Sun Yat-sen also warned the world, from the basis of what he understood as fundamental law, that if the proposed option would not be chosen, a new war would become inevitable.

History records that he was right. His words fell on deaf ears, and since the world did not respond to its own great need, as a consequence, the second world war erupted, the Cold War afterwards, and in China, Mao Zedong's cultural revolution created a self-escalating economic and social catastrophe that caused as many deaths over its period than World War II had caused in all aspects put together. The total may be above the 100 million mark, nearing 150 million deaths, if not more.

Again, Jesus' words were justified, pointing to the principle he illustrated, when he said: "This do, and thou shalt live."

In today's world, the principle that Christ Jesus understood, which is promoted again by Lyndon LaRouche and his organization, stands in opposition to the Aristocratic processes that very few people throughout history had cared to defend themselves against. For many years Lyndon LaRouche stood alone on this account. Except, now, during 1997, he is finding some faint response as people are beginning to recognize the validity of the principle that Christ Jesus has illustrated, that became in 15th Century the principle for the Renaissance and everything that came out of it, which Lyndon LaRouche has been promoting now for over 25 years. In the face of the presently unfolding world-financial disintegration, which he has foreseen several decades ago, he points to the utility of the historically demonstrated principles and says with the authority of a scientist: "This do, and thou shalt live."

Actually, he does more then this. He took on the role of the Samaritan, perhaps without knowing it, but by the force of the principle itself, and intervened actively in the political landscape of the world towards human development, opposing Aristocratic devolution. Some count it as arrogance when he points out that he is currently the only person qualified to intervene on behalf of humanity during the breakdown phase of the Aristocratic system, the present world-financial system. He points out that any failure to resolve by replacing the defective system will take the world down into a new dark age.

History may prove him right. There are no Samaritans to be found on the official world-political scene of today. While more and more people agree that his prior projections have all come true, there is no one on the political front who understands the Samaritan's principle that he represents, which would subsequently allow him to steer the course to save civilization and the life of vast portions of humanity.

The Aristocracy fears him most and does its utmost to discredit him. It's stooges even jailed him for 5 years. The Aristocracy wants the world deindustrialized and the human population reduced by four to five billion people, which it has committed itself to achieve through artificially created poverty and devolution. At is an irony of history, that this at this most critical juncture in the history of mankind, as the global system by which humanity lives is disintegrating, that one finds so little response among humanity in support of the man who fights for the life of humanity and its civilization.

Another irony of history is that Christ Jesus, who grew out of the renaissance of the Greek Classical Period, some 2000 years ago, understood our modern world better than it is understood in what is supposed to be a scientific age. He understood that the elite of the world is too bankrupt, spiritually, to stand up for humanity. He also understood that the same must be expected of the broader society that has elevated itself into positions of power and economic might, based on Aristotle's despicable concepts of natural slavery that justified the enslavement of mankind. Thus, Christ Jesus, evidently understood that the likelihood for uplifting the social scene would be far greater coming from those who stand worlds apart from the 'poverty' of the rich and the 'impotence' of the powerful.

Some say that Lyndon LaRouche's involvement in world-affairs is interfering in other people's domains. Some even say that the Samaritan did interfere in the same manner, that he should have walked by on the other side like the priest and Levite had done before him, and let the injured man die rather then raising him up. At least this is what the Aristocracy is saying, while it is doing all it can to deepen the injuries.

Indeed, non-interference has become a ploy of modern political correctness. It acts as a screen behind which destructive efforts are protected. The U.N. preached this ploy during the Serb aggression that destroyed Yugoslavia, actively preventing the attacked people from mounting a meaningful defense against their aggressors. Thus, the U.N., which has become an arm of Aristocratic policy, protected the slaughter of defenseless populations. Since there was no outcry against this policy the game has escalated and taken on ever more horrible forms in Africa.

# Chapter 1 - China and Spirituality

In today's world the protection of human rights has again been chosen as a ploy to protect the most viciously destructive world-political games that were ever launched in history, which is the game that aims at the destruction of two of the 'largest' nations on the planet, which are China and the U.S.A.. The depth of the game can only be understood when one recognizes the economic and financial position of China in the global context, and its vital importance for the survival of civilization.

China, is one of the last financially viable and economically functioning nation on the planet and is strongly pursuing ties for economic development with many nations of the Eurasian continent, especially those along the Eurasian Land Bridge that is already connecting China with Western Europe. China is presently poised, if its submission to western slavery is scrapped, to become the primary development engine for the entire Eurasian continent, which puts it on a collision course with the British Empire and its dying world-financial and economic system that is destroying the rest of the world.

The Empire sees a great threat in the developing potential of China, and it sees an even greater threat in the possibility that China and the U.S. become development partners and form a political and economic union. If this union were to take place, the capability would become unlocked to create an entirely new world-economic system that would force the present British imperial system through a bankruptcy reorganization and shut it down. This, the British Empire, is determined not to allow. The Empire, though it is no longer called that, needs its feudal financial system with which it is looting the world. Thus, an all-out hidden war has been launched by the Empire against China, being waged throughout the world. For this reason a special war has been launched to sour the once well-developed U.S.-Chinese cooperative relationship. The evident goal is to destroy both nations together by turning the targeted nations into adversarial positions for the purpose of engaging them into a war against each other, which many times before had been successfully accomplished.

The present offensive against China is carried forward on the human rights front, where China is being systematically hammered with accusations of gross violations, or intent of violations. Naturally, the recently mounted offensive against the existing cooperative Chinese-U.S. relationship, becomes an urgent thing with the Empire. It requires speedy results, because the disintegration of the world-financial system is near at hand, and with China's cooperation on the plate, Lyndon LaRouche's proposal for a New Bretton Woods type international monetary system could become a reality over night that would shut the British system down.

As it stands, Lyndon LaRouche's proposal is already being supported in many nations around the world, of which China is a key player. Without its participation, nothing can happen on the financial front. One should have no illusion about this: That without China there will be no New Bretton Woods type global financial reorganization for productive development, and without the proposed New Bretton Woods type world-financial recovery, many millions of people may not survive to the end of the century. Humanity should entertain no illusions about the consequences should the current imperial measures succeed in sabotaging the U.S. China relationship and thereby prevent the proposed New Bretton Woods conference from becoming a reality. When this happens, the disintegration of the world-financial system can no longer be prevented. Then, the present day poverty, ethnic strife, and terrorism that is ruling much of the world under the guiding hand of the Empire, may seem like a holiday by comparison.

The present world-financial system has long ceased to aid humanity. It has been destroying it step by step, and has itself become highly unstable by the same process. It needs to be taken down intelligently before it disintegrates, in order that the nations can be protected, that pensions can be saved, industries remain operational, food and energy supplies continue to be delivered, and social order be maintained. In an uncontrolled global systemic disintegration of the entire world-wide financial conglomeration, nothing can be protected.

So it is, that the lives of countless millions hang in the balance in a world-political game that is currently run against the U.S. and China under the cover of protecting human rights.*5

When Christ Jesus illustrated the natural manifestation of spirituality with his parable of the Samaritan, he failed to take into account the process that had caused the injury which the Samaritan addressed. He simply said that a traveler had fallen among thieves and was left by the wayside nearly dead. This man represents humanity.

Humanity is not quite at this point yet, nor can it

be determined how many people will survive the anarchy when the world-financial disintegration should come about. For those who may not survive the ensuing anarchy, the parable of the Samaritan is irrelevant. Spirituality, therefore, must salvage the scene at the present stage, before the disintegration begins. Unfortunately, there is little evidence of the existence of the required spirituality that will carry the day.

None can be found on the side of the Empire either, which aims to injure mankind under a cover of lies. Nor can any spirituality be found in the public's reaction to the imperial game. The initial reaction of the public has been to play along with the imperial game. All the Empire's assets and stooges in legislatures and other organizations promote the Empire's game of destruction with great force, and no one counters them, except in some isolated cases. Such a dramatic potential exposure to chaos renders the modern society fundamentally unfit for survival.

When Christ Jesus presented the face of spirituality by example and said "This do, and thou shalt live" he was evidently fully aware of what he was talking about. The alert action of the Samaritan that he presented, was evidently an act of self-preservation. Without building an environment of mutual support and protection, no one is safe.

In today's world the entire parable must be shifted forward a notch. We cannot wait until the world financial and economic system disintegrates. We need to address the injury of mankind that has already occurred, that began when the economic foundation for mankind was being demolished by escalating imperial demands and its ideologies, manifest in speculation, deindustrialization, and depopulation. The Samaritan must address this injury if he is to address anything at all. Unfortunately, whoever does this will find himself mostly alone, as society has chosen not to address itself to the problem, but has chosen to walk by on the other side.

In his exploration of the policies that have brought the world into the present era of free-trade slavery, deindustrialization, and economic and financial collapse, even to the point that the whole system is close to becoming unglued, Lyndon LaRouche has come to attribute the problem to the British Empire and its ideologies. With this established, he aims to free mankind from the influence of this Empire by shutting it down, just like William von Wolzogen had managed to shut down Napoleon's invasion of Russia. Indeed, this commitment is an essential element before any healing can begin, because before healing begins, the process of inflicting jury upon society must stops. And still, more than this is needed. In order to achieve this task, mankind

must first heal itself, and reestablish its spirituality in order to bring itself into a horizontal relationship with its most advanced leadership, the only real leadership that really exists.

Sadly, one sees little interest for this in today's society. Mankind has been taught well to ignore its plight, and walk in utter disregard of its own pain. This has become the norm.

This universal disinterest in spiritual principles, if one can still call it disinterest, is not natural. It has been artificially generated. In Christ Jesus' parable the Samaritan represents the natural reaction. Whatever reflects spirituality is the natural reflection of human nature, because man is a spiritual being. If this spirituality is missing, so that the only person who still stays the course becomes an isolated leader, then something is deeply wrong and humanity is grave danger.

To develop, to protect, to uplift, are the natural tendencies of man. By it, mankind has worked its way out of the stone ages. During the last two centuries, this natural tendency has been artificially reversed. Today, people are told that the level of prosperity that was once achieved, it can no longer be repeated - we have no money. The irony is, that money is not a natural resource that can be depleted. It is entirely an artificial product. Poverty is artificially created by an intentional dislocation of this artificial resource for the 'benefit' of those who have to power to do so. The Venetian merchant oligarchy had developed this process into a fine art. This oligarchy existed by clever processes of stealing, because its island bound existence did not allow large scale productive enterprises.

This policy of clever stealing grew out of the useful process of mercantile trading, which became more and more exploitative, increasingly high handed, until it became escalated into outright financial looting. This is the background out of which the British Empire was born after the Venetian's left their home base, and transplanted themselves to the north. The new Empire's highest public relations priority, of course, has always been to protect its practice of looting, later called "privilege" of looting. Today, the oligarchy has given itself the privilege to control the world's money supply and to impose its interest demands at will to its best advantage, no matter who is hurt thereby.

As a self-protective gesture, the Empire even allows society to take part in the game, to some degree, to legitimize the process. This is how the tendency was created to regard the Samaritan's response as unnatural, as exceptional. Some may even call it foolish. This is also how the tendency developed that prevents society from defending itself. When society is told that poverty is necessary because there is no money, no one disagrees. It stands ready to lay itself down to die, rather than to assert its spirituality and develop, protect, and uplift itself, by creating its own money as is needed for the necessary development to take place that assures its continued existence. Ironically, instead of doing this, the modern society literally looks away from its own plight.

This ironic tendency is a cleverly cultured effect created by the British Empire that has become the greatest feudal Empire on the planet. Its financial system has become the global system. Its system is doomed to disintegrate, just as Napoleon was doomed the moment he set foot on Russian soil. In either case, the large scale looting that is required to support the system cannot be carried out indefinitely without destroying the host that supports the parasitism, which has now become global in scale.

Still, the primary failure lies in the society's own neglect of the spirituality that is so fundamental to its civilization and existence. It must even be said that society would gain nothing if it could miraculously eliminate the forces of the Empire. Without spirituality to motivate its self-development, and its natural self-protection, even its scientific self-ennoblement, any society would continue to be fascist and imperially oriented in its pursuits, and embrace looting as a legitimate process for individuals to advance themselves.

The reverse must therefore also be true, namely that a society has the means within its grasp to protect itself at any time, against such an onslaught, and against the underlying destructive ideologies that have become accepted. All that society needs to do, is to promote its native spirituality. Then it will naturally act to protect itself and not walk by on the other side of the human need, but will act wisely.

One can expect, therefore, that today's ruling Empire, or other empires, will remain a part of the world scene until the natural spirituality of society is asserting itself, which, then, naturally obsoletes an oligarchy's existence. Whether there exists enough spiritual strength among mankind, today, to avert the currently impending crisis, cannot be determined. Spirituality can unfold quickly in times of crisis when the impediments are removed for the natural spirituality of mankind to assert itself. It is totally possible for the world scene to diverge quickly from the century old patterns of the past and gain a proper perceptions of itself.

# Chapter 2 - Processes That Enable Spirituality

We had previously examined the effects of regression in spirituality, as spirituality became smothered. We had examined it against the background of the Roman period. Let us now examine the opposite process, an increase in spirituality judged against the background of our own time.

One example can be found in Lyndon LaRouche's work. Through his studies of the classical geniuses, such as Wilhelm Leibnitz and Bernhard Riemann, an understanding of the dynamics of the human economy began to develop. This had put him at odds with the prevailing post war policies and its advocates, especially those of the later years, such as the policies represented by Henry Kissinger and George Bush of the late Cold War period. The Cold war had developed into a monster that increasingly threatened to end human existence in a global holocaust that could be set off within minutes. The doctrine of Mutually Assured Destruction was embraced as the keeper of the peace, but its credibility was wearing thin. With the discovery of the electromagnetic pulse effect, turned into a weapon, a first strike attack suddenly had a chance of being successful by disabling the opponent's missiles on the ground, preventing a retaliatory strike.

In order for the society to protect itself in this environment of a vastly increased vulnerability, it became self-evident to LaRouche that an active defense was needed. Based on his breakthrough discoveries in economic dynamics, he understood fully that such a defense could be achieved. He understood that with the development of new physical principles, such as the nuclear pumped x-ray laser that was developed for this purpose, mankind has the resources with itself to create the capacity to defend itself against these evermore indefensible missile threats. His idea of the technology based self-defense principle became eventually adapted by U.S. President Regan under the heading of the Strategic Defense Initiative.

Lyndon LaRouche also knew that the task was of such magnitude that no single country could succeed in this field, working by itself. In order for the project to succeed, both the Soviet's and the West, would have to cooperate technologically. So it was, that through back-channel discussions with the Soviets, invited by the president, the possibility for a cooperative development was explored. LaRouche made it clear that by such a system all cities could be protected.

As it was, the Soviet's refused to agree. Lyndon LaRouche predicted, that in such a case, by trying to do it alone, the Soviets would wreck their economy in five years or less, as they couldn't possibly take on such a momentous task by themselves. Not even the U.S. could do so, alone.

History proved him right. The Soviets wrecked their economy and their country within the time he predicted. At the end of the fifth year after Lyndon LaRouche's proposal the Soviet Union collapsed. He knew from his studies in economic dynamics, that one way or another, the Cold War would end under the force of this idea. In response to his idea, and his involvement, which quite probably saved the world, he was targeted by the Soviets whose plans he had spoiled, and by the Empire that had created the Cold War in the first place, so that he became convicted of totally irrelevant drummed up criminal charges and railroaded into prison.

It cannot be said that Lyndon LaRouche had seen the need of mankind and walked by on the other side. This might be said of much of humanity, which he tried to inspire to acknowledge its inherent strength and resources. And even in the absence of a response to his urging, he still benefitted the whole of humanity. In this case, the spiritual power of an idea, of one man, transformed the world.

From a technical standpoint he was railroaded into prison at the bidding of Henry Kissinger and the Soviet Union. In real terms he was convicted by the disinterest of the society with its own pain, and its refusal to acknowledge its development potential. By this refusal, mankind has literally convicted and doomed itself. As of this writing, the nuclear weapons threat is as ominous as it has ever been, if not more so. Most of the monster weapons of the Cold War period still exist. They are currently maintained under austerity conditions against the background of a disintegrating world-financial system, with a large portion being maintained in a country that is physically disintegrating towards civil war and a growing hatred of the West. Neither has mankind even begun to think about in earnest to develop an active defense system against these weapons, or to cooperate in removing them. For as long as inflicting injury is on the global agenda, which the Empire promotes with all its might, and world-wide economic development is actively prevented, neither of these options can be implemented.

Another example of Lyndon LaRouche's involvement to aid humanity took shape at the time when the Soviet empire collapsed. Even in the darkness of his prison cell he developed a plan by which the defeat of the Soviet Empire could be turned into a golden opportunity to create the most far reaching economic development project in history. This plan would uplift the entire Eurasian continent into an era of never before realized prosperity which would invariably uplift the entire world. The industrial engine to start such a vast development was recognized to exist ready made in the central regions of western Europe. Here, the British Empire stepped in, as it stepped in the last time that such a development scheme was proposed in the late 1800s. This time the British Empire succeeded in destroying this awesome development potential by throwing the entire continent into a dark age under its IMF's dictated brutal austerity demands. Today, the Russian economy, which would have been a powerful development contributor, lies in ruins, and the West European economies that could have provided the driving force of this development, have been reduced to beggars by the same IMF austerity demands. Thus, the brightest development opportunity in history was prevented, and the continental scene was turned into a nightmare of social chaos and starvation.

Being locked up in jail, as Lyndon LaRouche was at the time, he lacked the freedom to promote his vital idea. As a consequence of this missed opportunity fascism has gained the upper hand throughout much of the affected region.

# Chapter 3 - The Consequence of Walking By

Christ Jesus' parable of the Samaritan presents a highly simplified version of the principles of reality. It shows the contrast, but not the conflict between spirituality and the carriers of fascism. In fact, it doesn't show the face of fascism at all, except in the fate of the traveler. LaRouche had suffered this fate, and mankind had more than walked by on the opposite side as it observed the workings of a criminal justice system that has become criminal itself. Out of fear of this very system, many people are walking by on the other side. But what has the price been for this lack of spirituality? The price has been horrendous. The price has been the loss of the greatest era in economic prosperity in the history of mankind, which lay definitely within reach. The further result has been the destruction of Yugoslavia, the destruction of Iraq, genocide upon genocide in Africa, austerity and crime in Russia, and the economic devastation of the very industrial centers of Europe that could have served as the engine to kick-start a global economic development.

Today, the story has not changed much, although millions upon millions march in the streets of Europe in protest of their lost jobs and opportunities. However, as they march, none are realizing that they protest against the very result that their own lack of spirituality had directly occasioned. Neither do they bring forward a scientifically sound development plan that could turn their depression into prosperity. Instead, they merely protest. Still, this huge wave of protest is a faint step forward. Mankind has become inclined to stop walking by. While there is no sign yet of any "oil" or "wine" being poured into the wounds of injury, the society has begun to become alive.

A rule can be drawn up from these occasions, which states that any nation or society which lacks spirituality is fundamentally unfit for survival. Without spirituality fascism reigns, and under fascism no one can long survive. But the spark of spirituality also exists and has the tendency to assert itself when the fascism of the night becomes too imposing.

After Lyndon LaRouche was released from prison on parole, he devoted his efforts to help resolve the two major points of crisis that erupted out of this lost opportunity by mankind to initiate its self-development and security. One of these crisis was the genocidal war in Yugoslavia that had destroyed this nation and was unfolding into genocide. The other crisis was the accelerating collapse of the world financial system.

The war in Yugoslavia was easily addressed once the victimized people of Bosnia and Croatia could be helped to understand for whose 'benefit' this war had been unleashed. That this war was orchestrated for an economic strategic goal is self-evident if one considers the location of the country as a natural transportation corridor between western Europe, India and China, and Arabia and Africa. Once it was understood by the warring factions that the conflict had been set up to prevent economic development, and that the ensuing genocide was initiated to take the world's attention off the economic destruction that was moving in the background, enforced by the imperial oligarchy, and that the warring factions only served as willing pawns in a terribly destructive game, it became possible for Croatia and Bosnia to band together and defend themselves, thereby ending the nightmare. Armed with this understanding, a united effort was made, and the war ended in short order.

It was rather amazing to see how effectively the so motivated people were able to defeat their heavily armed opponents, often literally with their bare hands, until NATO finally stepped in and finished the job.

Their victory was won on a platform of spirituality. In this case the process was centered on the recognition of the truth, and on a heightened sense of self-appreciation that led to decisive action.

# Chapter 4 - The World-Financial Collapse

As mentioned before, the greatest peril that mankind is facing, has not been resolved as of this writing. The collapse of the world-financial system continues. It continues to collapse at an ever-accelerating rate towards a global systemic disintegration. Financial speculation has grown into a devastating giant. The whole of the Western society is reeling under its influence. The nations have become impoverished by it. They have been made poor and impotent by their own love of money. They can certainly see the destruction it causes as social support structures become eliminated, hospitals become closed, research becomes eliminated, the cost of education becomes put on the shoulders of the children themselves, industries become destroyed, food supplies become disrupted, infrastructures become neglected, etc. etc.. Still, they closed their eyes to the effects of this creeping fascism that has been implanted into their own axiomatic reactions, and so they walk by on the other side. At least they have done so until recently.

LaRouche's calls for a tax on speculation, that would largely eliminate speculation, have been ignored. Calls for taking the system through an orderly reorganization, in order that development can take place again, have been smothered. His latest initiative, a call for a New Bretton Woods conference, is but spasmodically heeded. His call is presently supported by some of the most severely effected countries, reeling under the IMF austerity dictates. Unless some strong movement begins in this arena that causes a decisive shift from fantasy to reality, mankind will likely loose this final opportunity, also, to re-organize and develop itself. The crisis that mankind is moving towards as its financial system is breaking down, portents to be the potentially worst physical crisis in its entire existence, which will erupt the moment when its world-financial system disintegrates. Against this crisis that mankind is speeding towards at full steam, very little resistance is put up by which it might save itself. Lyndon LaRouche stands once again virtually alone at the leading edge of this front, struggling against the power of the Empire and the global apathy of mankind, hoping that a breakthrough opening somewhere will provide an opportunity for him to shift the tide.

Right now, the time to maneuver is running out rapidly. Also the need for LaRouche's exoneration, and that of his associated who are still incarcerated, is becoming of paramount importance. With a criminal conviction hanging over him, no matter how unjust and politically motivated it was, his effectiveness is hampered. In fact, it closes the doors to such places of public service where his involvement in times of a crises might become crucial. Mankind cannot afford to loose this support when it is most needed, nor can the Empire afford to relent from its persecution which is crucial for the success of its games. Right now, the society has chosen to play the Empire's card, with which it is playing against its own most vital interests.

What conditions will prevail when a world-wide systemic financial disintegration occurs, in which the banking system disintegrates and money looses its value, cannot be imagined, much less be prepared for. Right now the banks' exposure in derivatives gambling is many times greater than their depositors' equity, and vastly greater than the banks' own equity. Right now the banks reap huge profits from this process, in which they literally bet the bank that the markets don't go against them. But in a breakdown crisis this tends to reverse itself and the banks loose many times what they have. Since the entire financial world is so tightly interlocked with interlocking speculation, and so highly super-inflated in comparison to the real world, the probably is extremely high that the whole thing becomes unhinged simultaneously within a matter of two or three days in which everything related to money looses its value.

How a society functions in such a case; how it procures and transports food to the cities without money, and distributes the food; how it procures fuels for transportation and processing, with nothing to pay in exchange; how it maintains the essential services for public order and personal security, cannot be determined. No city on the planet carries enough supplies to maintain itself for more than a couple of weeks. In Germany, after Hitler's Reich was defeated in war, it took quite a few weeks to set up a new economic system. People were eating charcoal from burnt out buildings to get something at all in their stomachs. And this happened at a time when the rest of the world was in infinitely better shape than it is today. How long the recovery period will be when the entire world is in crisis is anybody's guess. Nor can the scope of the anarchy be determined that is certain to unfold.

How many people will perish in such an event may be determined by the Empire. The Empire has been lobbying for decades for a dramatic population reduction. It may hope for a global death toll of between two and five billion people. One must assume that the Empire will likely do everything in its power to prevent a speedy recovery from such a crisis, which it has the capacity to control as it controls much of the world's monetary institutions and owns a high percentage of the international food distribution infrastructure. The injured man that the Samaritan encounters by the wayside is evidently humanity itself. Nor is it likely that the "priests" and "Levites" of today will act fundamentally different than Christ Jesus had illustrated in the parable.

Lyndon LaRouche refuses to speculate on how a global financial disintegration will effect the society. The consequences are too horrid to contemplate. He insists that they are irrelevant, as the war against the world-feudal system must be won before it disintegrates into chaos. He suggest that if the world-financial reorganization cannot be achieved before the thing disintegrates, or at the moment of its disintegration, everything that follows will be irrelevant. In the chaos of total anarchy, everything will indeed be irrelevant in the face of death.

What the Empire's position is, in its war against humanity, is evident by the intensity and how the game is run in its attack on China that is presently unfolding in ever greater fury a few months before the Chinese takeover of Hong Kong. According to available evidence, a major salvo in this attack on China will be synchronized to the repatriation of Hong Kong into the Chinese state. As of this writing there are plans in progress that will no doubt make the repatriation of Hong Kong as explosive as it can possibly be made. Towards this explosive end three major pieces of legislation are put before the U.S. Congress that would extend U.S. law into the domain of the Hong Kong China relationship with types of demands that a sovereign nation cannot possibly accept. The frightening this is, that this legislation will likely become law.

The anti-China legislation is designed to sail through the House and Senate on the wave of the whipped up anti-China hysteria that is currently generated in the imperially owned press and news media throughout the U.S. and much of the world. As a political event, the repatriation of Hong Kong into China has the potential to become a modern day replay of the 1914 political explosion in Sarajevo that lit the fuse for World War I and ended up destroying the life of over 50 million people in two of the most ugly wars in human history.

The Empire's staged assassination of Archduke Francis Ferdinant of the Austro Hungarian Empire, and his wife Sophy, that took place in Sarajevo on June 1914, was a minor event compared to the political demands that were tied to it in the aftermath that were so sweeping and enormous in nature that they could not possibly be met by any sovereign nation anywhere. The

same type of setup had been prepared in respect to China's resuming control over Hong Kong, which may yet be unleashed.

The real goal of the Empire's position against China, of course, has nothing to do with protecting human rights. That the Empire has no commitment to human rights is well demonstrated by its financial, political, and logistical support of international terrorism and genocide, especially in Africa; and by its support of the world-wide dope trade that is destroying the nations of the world from within; and also by its insistence on free trade slavery that has engulfed 250 million of the world's children into sweatshop servitude. The real goal of the Empire's move against China is the same that prompted it to setup World War I, which was staged to prevent the economic development of the Eurasian continent by means of a land-bridge transportation link from China to Europe. Today, thanks to China's economic power, this link has at long last become a reality with several more links now in the planning stage that will integrate Japan, Indonesia, India, Arabia, Africa, and Russia into the greatest economic development block ever imagined, if it is not crushed by the Empire. Ultimately the dynamics of the kind of continent wide economic development that is planned, will tie in North America via an all-weather road and rail link running through Yatusk in Siberia, across the Bering Strait to Alaska, from where it would intertie the Eurasian economic block with that of the American continent.

When the Empire moved against Europe to prevent this type of continent wide self-development, the Empire's economic house was in a mess, similar to today's, although in those early days its financial foundation was very far from disintegrating, not like we have it now. The Empire's move against China will therefore be pushed more strongly, and by all the forces the Empire can muster. Its war against China will be carried forward regardless of what happens to Hong Kong as the result of its repatriation.

The U.S. is presently drawn into the game against China. It is being set up as the West's major player to be pitted against the Asian giant. One can see in this move the replay of the diplomacy of King Edward VII who was able to maneuver the major powers of Europe into adversarial positions against each other that caused them to murder one another in an orgy of violence that superseded the worst in human history up to this time.

While China is being set up for a major salvo from the outside, involving the United States of America, it is simultaneously set up for internal explosions by means of already established ethnic separatist terrorism that had been instigated and supported by various channels of the British Empire. One of the most active of these separatist terrorist organizations is the so-called Uighur separatist movement that operates in China's Xinjian province that spans an important segment of the Eurasian Land-Bridge and development corridor. If the terrorist rampage succeeds in breaking the province away from China, which may well happen as there is strong imperial pressure and support behind this terrorist treachery, then the Empire will once again be in a position to destroy the greatest development potential of all times.

Nor is the Empire's campaign against China the only game in progress. In parallel to this, Mexico is being set up for an explosion from within. The Empire's servants in the U.S. legislator are pushing hard to have the U.S. adopt policies that "ferment chaos in Mexico" in order to crush the institutions, such as the ruling government, that stand in the way of the IMF demanded "reforms." Mexico's ruling party is termed irredeemably corrupt, as a pretext for it being removed with violence in the name of "democracy." It is demanded by U.S. legislators that the power of the Mexican Presidency and the military be slashed, and that in the name of the reform, Mexico's population (termed overpopulation) be drastically reduced. In other words, it is demanded that the institutions that hold the country together be eliminated, together with presumably large segments of Mexico's people.

One must assume from this that the resulting power vacuum would, then, be filled by drug trafficking terrorism that would find little resistance overflowing across the border into the southern U.S., opening a dope pipeline that may not be easily shut again. The opening salvo in this war against Mexico and the U.S. was narrowly avoided when under pressure from the White House the Senate refrained from joining the Mexico bashers on March 21, 1997. Except this slim victory of a narrow escape from chaos, does not mean that the war has been won. The ferment continues. It continues in the background to Mexico's growing financial and economic crisis, and in the background to the separatist terrorist pressures that push for splintering the Mexican nation into a number of ethnically bound mini-states that can be much more readily dominated by the Empire than a well functioning nation-state.

And again, China and Mexico are not the only games that the empire has in progress. Africa is deeply torn by these games. One of Africa's largest country, the Sudan, is set up to be torn apart by imperially bought invasions and political pressures. Zaire, too, will soon be history as its territory becomes added once against to the Empire's inventory. The Empire's colonial days have not ended in Africa, as its new colonial puppet nations now fight its wars, whose people supply the manpower for the imperial machine that is destined to steam-roll across the continent after Zaire and the Sudan have been assimilated into the Empire's system.

The region of the Middle East from Israel to Iran, including the Arab states, is another imperially controlled powder keg. There will be no peace in the region, no matter how many concessions are given for appeasement. The Empire needs to keep the fuse burning. If it didn't, it would loose control over the oil and allow this region to become the transportation hub between Europe, Africa, the Arab nations, and tie into the southern link of the Eurasian Land-Bridge across India, Indonesia, China, and the islands of Japan. The Empire has long demonstrated that it will not allow this type of economic development to take place anywhere in the world.

It is highly likely that the Empire will attempt to play its China, Mexico, Africa, and Middle East cards simultaneously around the time when the repatriation of Hong Kong occurs. It needs to drag the U.S. into a political quagmire and a possible confrontation on many fronts, because such a move would certainly put an end to any New Bretton Woods type monetary reordering. It knows that such a reordering would put an end to the hopelessly bankrupt imperial feudal monetary system that has become the world-financial system and the backbone of its prosperity. It knows that such a reordering will replace its feudal system with a development oriented system, and it knows that it must prevent this. It also knows that if it can prevent a New Bretton Woods monetary reordering from becoming a reality, it will not be defeated. For this it must drive especially the U.S. and China apart, into adversarial positions. Without China and the U.S. cooperating, there will be no financial reordering possible to power a global development. It will take the combined strength of the U.S. and China to obsolete the British system. The Empire knows that it cannot allow this strength to be achieved.

On many occasion in history, its clever diplomacy, centered on lies, has turned mankind's hope to dust, causing great injury. Such diplomacy has turned potential development partners into violent foes, who were then incited to destroy each other, such as in World War I. Creating havoc based on diplomatic lies has always been a special talent of the British Empire that goes back to the Empire's very conception and beyond. This 'talent' can be traced back to the Empire's roots in the Venetian Empire that had developed this method into a fine art for achieving political destruction.

# Chapter 5 - The Tragedy of Lies

How 'information' can effect the society is vividly illustrated by the 1997 scandal in the gold mining industry. When information was released that a Canadian mining company had discovered the richest gold deposits in the world on its properties in Indonesia, the value of its shares grew by leaps and bounds. When it became revealed later on that the information was false, the share value dropped to near zero, and then, recovered a bit. On the strength of this information billions of dollars were made and lost, and the lives of numerous people were irrevocably altered.

While the false information in the above case was probably not created intentionally for the purpose to cause injury, the power of lies has been employed on countless occasion in diplomacy for achieving destructive purposes. King Edward VII of the British Empire, the true architect of World War I, was an able diplomat in this respect who exploited the destructive effect of this process to the utmost in order to protect the Empire from the economic threat that the planned transportation land-bridge across Asia would create, that was to set up the world's largest economic development block, extending from Paris to Japan, including all of Asia in due course. Carefully crafted lies, intertwined with hyped up nationalism had suffice to turn the potential development partners at each other's throat.

Lies are possibly the most destructive weapons ever devised, and the most indefensible, as they cause the victim to engage in voluntary self-destruction. They are employed economically, politically, and financially.

In the financial realm, at the present moment, the illusion is spread across the world that stockmarket investment through mutual funds is a sure way to riches, even though the physical industry that this market represents is collapsing through disinvestment and politically motivated deindustrialization. The illusion that this market builds wealth has been created by the cleverly spread lies from which the architects of the game profit immensely. The illusion is so eagerly accepted that it is causing the society to throw all its savings and its liquid equity, even some borrowed money, into the sink hole from which it cannot be reclaimed. The modern financial market that exists by these lies, is without doubt the most monumental pyramid scheme ever invented, with a near unimaginable potential for injury.

Another set of lies, vastly more destructive than these, are those that are hidden under the cover of science. There are quite a number of them by now. Some of them are murdering millions of people every year, like those that caused the ban of DDT which had once nearly eradicated malaria around the world, that is back, and had effectively protected crops, which is no longer possible to the same degree.

The potentially most destructive of the scientific lies, however, is the one centered on the Global Warming scare that has been created as a weapon against mankind's fossil fuel energy use on which modern life depends. Nothing can replace fossil fuel energy in the world, for as long as nuclear energy development is actively impeded. Wind mills can't do it, nor can solar cells or bio-fuels that require more energy to produce than they give back. Nor can hydro power be developed into a significant energy source. Most existing potentials have already been developed. There is little more left in the wings. Therefore, with nuclear power development being actively impeded, the fossil fuel remain as the only energy resource mankind has. The entire world is powered by it.

If one considers the enormously destructive effect that a significant shut down of fossil fuel energy use is bound to have on the world population, it should not be surprising that one finds the originators of the Global Warming mythology to be the same imperial elite circles who also demand a massive world-population reduction. For decades upon decades the Empire has demanded a massive world-population reduction, that would, if it were implemented, create a more ideal environment for the feudalist system. But until recently, its bidding has been largely ignored. Now it is being wholly embraced. The project is now pursued under the cover of a lie. The lie is called Global Warming, that is being associated with a great scare of the polar ice caps melting and flooding low lying lands. Under this lie that few people have the resources to disprove a war is waged against fossil fuel energy use, while at the same time nuclear power development remains prevented. Thus, the real evident goal is to shut down, or dramatically curtail, mankind's energy production on which modern existence absolutely depends. The current 5.5 billion person world population simply cannot maintain itself in an energy lean environment. Take away the energy use that supports this population - that is needed to produce its food, power its transportation systems, drive its industries, heat its homes, cook its food, etc., and mankind will necessarily die back dramatically to a smaller population existing on a much more primitive platform. This is what the Global Warming mythology is intended to achieve.

Mathematically speaking, the strength of a civilization, expressed in population density, is in direct relationship to its energy production in general terms. The discovery of this interrelationship is one of Lyndon LaRouche's early achievements for which he has been internationally honored. Right now, humanity is playing the Empire's game, in that it is manipulating itself into a trap that is designed to destroy its food supply, its industry, and its transportation systems by volunteering to shut down its energy use on which its very existence depends as these infrastructures depend entirely on large scale energy production.

It is quite possible that billions of people will perish by this process that has now begun, or by similar processes. They may perish just as quietly as millions upon millions of people have already perished from the effects of scientific lies that resulted in the DDT ban.

The history of the scientific lie has had its beginning, most prominently in the Thomas Malthus, Charles Darwin, and Francis Galton era out which the Eugenics 'science' developed that had its most destructive manifest in Adolf Hitler's extermination of the Jewish population in his realm. This lie also did its dirty work on the American continent where it was reflected in racially oriented mass sterilizations and in such huge racially oriented mass movements as the infamous Ku Klax Klan.

In today's age the Empire's antipopulation deployment of science is no longer directly racially oriented. Rather, it has become universal in scope, and is directed against mankind's most vital infrastructures for living, such as its technologies for energy production, for protection from diseases, for food production, and for refrigeration. The Ozone Depletion scare, for instance, has already committed mankind to dramatically scale back its refrigeration capability, especially in the poorer nations. The death toll from this attack on humanity is expected to reach as high as 40 million people per year, world wide, once the CFC refrigerants are fully prohibited under the currently imposed ban.

The most powerful lies are those that are most deeply hidden, which thereby appear as truth. Ideological factors are frequently involved in both the creation of the lies and in their concealment. The services of science are often brought into the game to aid the concealment of ideologically contrived goals, and to impose the effect of a lie. This 'diversion' of science is easily accomplished with selective financial and political support for the agencies that lend themselves most readily to the game, and the judicial removal of those scientists from their post or status who stand up

for what is real. On the wings of money and political power science can become misused as a destroyer of civilization.

If one were to relate this tendency to the parable of the Samaritan, one would find the Samaritan not pouring "oil" and "wine' into the injured man's wounds, but poison.

# Chapter 6 - With the Intent to Injure

It is a sad thing that the society's trust in science is being so cruelly abused for destructive purposes, as one sees this happening today. By the glitter of its magic science inspires a trust that had been well disserved in the years when the intend of scientific enquiry was to discover the nature of reality and to apply the discovered principles for the advance of civilization. On this platform had all the technological infrastructures been created that support the modern civilization. Mankind's natural trust in the supportive nature of science, however, leaves it dangerously vulnerable to the abuse of science and scientific institutions as has become increasingly prevalent in the postwar period.

From historic times to the present day, mankind has not found it possible to establish a reliable active defense against lies. If it had achieved such a defense, the present century would not have unfolded as a century of wars.

The many more recent abuses of science for destructive games, reveals the deep deficiency that exists in mankind's self-defense against destructive manipulation. How can a society protect itself if the individual person lacks the resources to explore political conspiracies. Has had the average person of the society commanded the resources to explore the movements going on beneath the scene that unfolded into a tightly knit conspiracy which created World War I? The answer must be in the negative. This level of alertness did not exist anywhere in the world at this time. It doesn't even exist now. The society at large still has not found it prudent to scrutinize scientific data for deceptive distortions or clever misrepresentations, that underlie modern conspiracies, such as the ones that drive the Ozone Hole and Global Warming mythologies? It appears that not even Christ Jesus had developed an effective defense against these types of processes. One must assume that the Roman Empire had developed formidable skills in the art of deception, with which it protected its dominance. But Christ Jesus had said nothing about them, or had he?

If one considers the parable of the Samaritan one might notice that Christ Jesus had said more about this subject in this single parable than the modern society finds interest in pursing. Also, he did it in quite a dramatic manner. The parable opens with the statement that the unfortunate traveller was robbed, wounded, and left half dead by the wayside. Was it necessary for him to go deeper into the details and pursue how the man was robbed and wounded, whether it was accomplished with a sword, a knife, a club, or a stone, and whether or not the man defended himself bravely, or whether he fell into the trap of deception? The fact is, no matter by what process he was injured, the end result is the same in every case. The end result reflected the intend to injure, the rest is irrelevant.

Many people might disagree, here, and say that the intend of the thief was to enrich himself, and that inflicting injury was secondary. This reasoning is defective, because even a thief knows that his enrichment is fundamentally injurious. Theft inflicts injury. So, the motive was to injure.

The motive of spirituality, on the other hand, that the Samaritan represents, is to heal, to raise up, to develop the requisite strength that enables an injured individual to once again provide for himself. The motive of spirituality is to uplift, to protect, and to develop.

This duality in intend, that we find illustrated in the parable, invariably reflects itself in the corresponding duality in effect. The two are linked. One betrays the other. Christ Jesus clearly indicated that spirituality rests on the side were the intend is to raise up, to protect, to develop, where spirituality manifests itself in the corresponding effects.

The defective systems of our times betray themselves by the criteria that Christ Jesus has thereby established.

Let us expose the Global Warming myth to this criteria. Is there an intend to injure, or is there an intend to raise up, to protect, and to develop? An answer to this question can be found in the urging by the controllers of the game, who insisted that mankind should ignore the economic consequences of their demands, and fulfill these demands no matter what the cost in human lives may be. The intend, therefore, is to injure. Nothing changes the intend, even if the belief is that the injury is for a noble cause. Hitler used the same excuse. He caused the death of 50 million people in a global war, in pursuit of his noble case.

If the Samaritan of today was truly concerned about a global warming, and there existed demonstrable proof that global warming is occurring, and there was real scientific proof available that this warming is caused by increases in $CO_2$ levels in the atmosphere, and that these increases are demonstrably contributed exclusively by man-made sources even though the man made sources are minute compared to the natural sources of $CO_2$, how would the Samaritan have to react? Would he make the same demands for inflicting injury on mankind? Or might he not rather urge the speedy development alternate energy resources, such as nuclear power, no matter what the financial cost might amount to, in order that mankind may live and have a future? If he were concerned about nuclear fallout, accidents, or nuclear waste, he would note that all these concerns are already addressed by today's leading edge reactor technologies. And even if he was not satisfied with the leading edge safety standards, he would redouble efforts to solve the problems that remain. He would go to the greatest extend with this, but never consider taking the life-line away from humanity as it is being proposed toady.

Indeed, the shutting down of mankind's fundamental lifeline, is what is being demanded today under the Global Warming mythology. This is what it has been created for. And for what? Not a single one of the above listed points of the Global Warming mythology has been demonstrably proven. The entire mythology is based on a lie and is upheld by speculative conjectures and statistical and mathematical models that are subjective to what they are intended to proof. For this, mankind is demanded to reduce its civilization to the level of a primitive, energy lean existence similar to that of the dark ages while the presently available alternate energy technologies are violently suppressed. There is clear intend for injury involved in this approach, and not the slightest intend to raise up, to protect, and to develop.

---

# Chapter 7 - The Political Intent to Injure

It may be that the Empire will succeeds in its latest games in the political arena where one sees an all-out effort being made to pit the U.S. against China, Mexico against the U.S., the narco terrorists against Mexico, and the Chinese separatist terrorists against the nation of China itself. Also, China is surrounded with a ring of 'fires' in the form of artificially created conflicts for the destabilization of China by explosive external forces. Hong Kong, now that it has been integrated into the Chinese economy, may also be used by the British Empire to project its 'fire' directly into the heart of China by activating its economic imperial assets that have not left Hong Kong together with the British Garrisons on the day of the repatriation of Hong Kong.

It might be that the Empire won't score a single victory on any of these fronts, and that sanity will prevail. China is fully committed to doing everything possible to avoid a catastrophe. One needs to take notice, however, that if the Empire succeeds in setting the U.S. up against China before the (imperial) world-financial system can be reorganized - which can only succeed with China and the USA cooperating fully - there will be little left standing in terms of national powers that can hold back the British Empire's long cherished dream of a total global domination, and its far reaching global population elimination goal (termed overpopulation reduction) down to below the one billion level from the present world-population level of 5.5 billion people.

Those who manage to survive the ensuing murder by poverty and starvation, which is already in progress in Russia, North Korea, Africa, and some other IMF dominated nations, will face, not the dawn of a new utopia, but a 500 year period of dark ages bound to serfdom and slavery. This is what an imperial victory implies. This is what it will bring. This is what the old imperialism had brought until the Golden Renaissance in the 15th century had put an end to it. The renewal of spirituality that occurred, then, must be achieved gain, today, if the presently achieved civilization is to be protected.

China's greatest foe, therefore, is not the British Empire, in spite of the repeated and deep reaching destruction the Empire has brought upon China since the beginning of its dope smuggling operations and subsequent Opium Wars. China's greatest foe is ultimately its own self-isolation by which its momentous economic development stops at its border. It fails in meeting the test criterion that Christ Jesus has established with the parable of the Samaritan. It concerns itself far too little with the rest of the world and the chaos that surrounds it, so much so that it is effectively "walking by on the other side" as the high minded elite had done in Jesus' parable. The Samaritan, in the parable, supported the humanity that he valued, and in so doing he created the rich human environment that evidently wanted to live in. The priest and Levite, in spite of their riches as the elite, were to poor in the spiritual dimension to recognize the greater value that was in danger of becoming lost, that they made every effort to ignore.

The world is full of priests and Levites, today. The Empire's GATT, Free-Trade, IMF process breeds them in great numbers. We find them in America, Europe, Asia, and Africa. We find them in the highest places, announcing proudly that in the course of their new globalism some nations become "marginalized" as an inevitable consequence. Thus, a hundred million people are **allowed** to die each year from forced underdevelopment and related causes, which includes the unnecessary death of 33,000 children under the age of five each single day. There are only a precious few Samaritans found in modern history. One was President Delanor Roosevelt, who had put forward a strong commitment to devote the built up industrial might of the United States of America, that has supplied the economic power for winning World War II, to achieve the rapid industrialization and economic development of the world. Unfortunately he died, supposedly of natural causes, at the very moment at which this commitment as to begin in uplifting the world.

Another Samaritan in modern history was President John Fitzgerald Kennedy who had established a policy platform that was destined to lead to world economic development. He was murdered long before these policies could be carried out. In later years the leaders of Japan proposed to do the same, after the Industrial development of Japan had reached a high point, but was prevented for doing so under the threat that Japan would no longer be covered by the American nuclear umbrella.

As a result of eliminating their Samaritans, the respective nations, and indeed the world, suffered unspeakable losses. Without Roosevelt's commitment to global development, the USA and the world was drawn into the nightmare of a nuclear confrontation that nearly destroyed humanity and civilization as a whole. Without

Kennedy's similar commitment to world industrialization and development, which ended with his assassination, the USA and the world became drawn into one of the most powerful dehumanization in history, that the Vietnam war became. Without Japan's commitment to third-world development in later years, that was eliminated almost at gunpoint, the economic strength of Japan was redirected to inflate the worldwide real estate bubble that nearly destroyed Japan's banking system, when it popped, and caused untold financial damage throughout the world.

The principle that Christ Jesus illustrated with the parable of the Samaritan is one of the fundamental principles that cannot be ignored without dire consequences. Right now, China's spirituality is put to the test, and as far as can be determined, it is found wanting. By this failure, the currently brightest star of humanity is in danger of becoming extinguished again. The political and psychological forces that are currently arrayed against China are immense. They can only be negated by a policy aimed at changing the world and uplifting humanity with developing the kind of economic prosperity that reflects the dignity of the human being as the brightest manifest in the arena of life on this planet.

In our modern age, the final vestige of mankind's last period of Renaissance, the nation-state, and that nations that have developed a high stated of civilization on this platform, are being set up to be destroyed. If this destruction occurs, the cycle will be over in which the Renaissance had enabled mankind to escape from poverty and serfdom for half a millennium, which became, in spite of all its problems and trials, an epoch filled with near universal prosperity, freedom, great art, music, and scientific advances such as the world had not seen before this Renaissance occurred.

The only defense that mankind has against the already mounted assault against itself, is it's spirituality. With the parable of the Samaritan, Christ Jesus has set a mirror before humanity in which it can judge itself and its prospects for maintaining its civilization and to a large degree its existence. Before this century ends, the parable of the Samaritan will gain its most profound significance ever, as mankind is forced to make clear distinctions between the processes driven by those who aim to injure it in the most sweeping fashion, and the intend of those who aim to uplift, protect, and develop its potential. On this choice that will be made in today's age, intelligently or by default, before the current century ends, hangs mankind's future for the next 5-10 centuries, if not forever. Will mankind be wise enough to choose life over death, as Christ Jesus had suggested that a choice in favor of spirituality involves? This is the great and all-overriding question that humanity is facing today.

There is one interesting element in the parable of the Samaritan that has rarely been applied to the political scene, but which is especially important in the present age. It is an element that has been applied only once in a major fashion. This element is found in the Samaritan's financial support of the injured man. The Samaritan gave the innkeeper whatever was required for the injured man's recovery, including a continuing provision with the promise that he would recompense the innkeeper should additional needs in his recovery arise. This kind of support is sadly lacking, today, in every conceivable respect, although history tells us that this was not always the case.

In a somewhat remote sense, perhaps, this type of supportive process was found most prominently in India. It was found in support of Mohandas Gandhi, who had stood up for the rights of the nation and had stood his ground against the might of the British Empire as a colonial power. On the strength of the support that this man received, which was well disserved, Gandhi had in time inspired the entire nation to stand its ground against the British Empire, and had enabled it to be victorious in the end.

In this case the Indian nation, as a whole, had assumed the role of the Samaritan. Without its support for its most advanced pioneer for freedom, its freedom would have never been won. Gandhi defense for the dignity of man, which could only be non-violent, was India's self-defense. The power of this process was so dramatic that it inspired almost universal support for India's independence, even from afar.

Gandhi had studied British law and, then, came to South Africa to practice it. There, he found this law so immensely repressive of the rights of the people as human beings, that he fought for the victims of the law. When Gandhi returned to India in 1915, his fame in this fight for so great a cause, was such that was he was hailed as "mahatma" a "great soul." This identity became ever after attached to his name as a spiritual identifier. It was associated with him in a similar fashion in which the term Christ became attached to the name of Jesus.

In a documentary on Mahatma Gandhi it was disclosed that the people's elite of India had decided virtually from the start that it must support this man with whatever financial means were required, which were rather modest indeed, but sufficient for the task. In contrast, one finds little of this type of support in modern times, in America for instance. Lyndon LaRouche, there, who presently fights the battle in this age against the destructive forces of the British Empire, receives extremely little in terms of financial support that compares in any way to the scope of the task he is facing. His research into history and economics has established Lyndon LaRouche as apparently today's foremost opponent of the British Empire, its financial looting of the world, and its modern world-political games that are costing mankind a tall price in human lives. When he was confronted with a choice in the 1980s, he had chosen to risk being conflicted and cast into prison rather than stopping his fight for humanity. Mankind should count itself fortunate for the efforts of this man, and that of his associates who are few, instead it chooses to revile and slander to negate the very policy imperatives on which the welfare of society ultimately depends.

One finds a historic irony in this, and a dramatic departure from all previous efforts by mankind to uplift itself out of the mire of imperial domination. In previous times, mankind's Samaritans have been eliminated by the Empire itself by various methods of assassination. Now the Empire has managed, by means of its near total control of the world's media, and with it, its near total control over the mental processes of society, to cause society to persecute its own pioneers and make their efforts more potently ineffective than assassination could have achieved.

This contrast between the support that Gandhi had received in India, and the lack of such support for Lyndon LaRouche who has devoted his life to a much greater and more urgent task than Gandhi had, is interesting and portents to a danger to society that may soon become indefensible.

The contrast appears to be indicative of an underlying factor that existed richly in India, but which can no longer be found to any significant degree in the modern Western World. This factor is, evidently, spirituality. The people of India had been able to muster the required support for their most advanced pioneer, as their spirituality had been traditionally strong. The people of India have had quite a long history in certain types of nationally oriented spiritual exploration, while the western word has become increasingly fascinated with evermore advanced processes of stealing from each other to the point that the development of the society's potential is no longer regarded a vital factor.

The spiritual factor has been rendered dormant in the modern Western society bent on speculation, violence, looting and illusions. While Lyndon LaRouche receives some support at the grass roots level of society, this support falls short by a long measure to what is reasonable for the scope of the task at hand that no one else has chosen to pursue. This lack of support by the society for its leading edge pioneers who aim to protect, uplift, and develop the great potential of the modern society, translates itself into the society's utter lack of support for itself. This lack of support may very well cost mankind immeasurably in the years to come. In today world all the support is thrown into the arena of destructive pursuits, conservatism, and shutting mankind down by means of poverty and starvation.

Huge sums are spent for destructive goals, primarily by the Empire and its vast networks of agents and agencies, on destructive operations that undermine the physical existence and the spirituality of the nations, rather than in support of strengthening the physical infrastructures and the spirituality that are so essential for the society's existence.

In the face of this vastly counterproductive effort, the mirror that Christ Jesus has set up for mankind to judge itself, projects a horrid foreboding for its future. Still, Christ Jesus was not only an advocate of spirituality, but was also an outstanding healer. He demonstrated that the society's worst diseases can be overturned at an instant. Within the parameters of advanced spirituality, he demonstrated that it is possible for mankind to heal itself, to reawaken its spirituality. This is what the book series "Discovering Infinity" has been intended to accomplish. The reward for success in this arena is life. As Christ Jesus had pointed out, "This do, and thou shalt live."

Now, how can one be sure that spirituality is a factor, and that the policies of Lyndon LaRouche for universal economic development are the right ones for this age? After all, at the present time Lyndon LaRouche's voice is the only one that can be heard in defense of scientific, technological, and industrial development. The rest of the world talks about down-sizing, deindustrialization, and free-trade magic. As for the disintegrating world-financial system, again, his is the only voice that warns about an escalating threat, and the warnings could be heard since the 1970s, long before the first big tremors were felt on the financial scene. And even now, after ten major tremors have hit since 1994 (Orange County - 1994; Mexico - 1994; Barings - 1995; Sumitomo - 1995; Credit Lyonnais, 3rd bailout - 1996; Japan - 1996/97; Thailand - 1996/97; Korea - 1996/97; Belgian govmt.- 1997; Germany - 1996/97) the real explosions are only beginning. Before 1997 drew to a close the much lauded "Asian Tiger" economies died almost over night and Japan saw two of its biggest financial institutions slide into bankruptcy. No one else besides Lyndon LaRouche and his associates had warned of these tremors as the consequence of an escalating universal financial speculation binge, coupled with a collapse of the physical economy towards a global economic disintegration.

Some of the leading 'experts' in financial circles

begin to admit that LaRouche was right to some degree as they begin to see today's massive problems erupting all over the place, but none of them agree with him on what he recognizes as the only possible solution. Most people insist that one mustn't touch what drives speculation in the markets that have registered unprecedented gains over the last couple of years. Only a few recognize instinctively that this fairy tale world of assumed riches that were never created in real terms, can't go on forever, and therefore won't. But gripped with a fear of loosing the ground they believe has been gained, the self-enlightened are not willing to consider what Lyndon LaRouche puts forward as the only logical and fundamental solution. Therefore they make every effort to patch up the failing system with evermore Band-Aids and duct tape, adding injury to poverty, and then join the chorus of those who call LaRouche an extremist.

The irony is, that the man is anything but an extremist. From a scientific point of view it must be said that his proposed solutions do actually fall short of what is really needed. He presents technical aspects for economic development and financial solutions that support development. These may not be implementable without a revitalization of the society's spirituality. In fact, the proposed solutions that he calls for are a manifest of the man's own rich spirituality, which require a certain equivalent base to be understood and implemented. When the financial elite becomes confronted with his proposals, it sees merely the technical side of them, which it considers extreme. Indeed, it must consider them so, as it recognizes only half of what must be achieved to make the proposals implementable.

Now, before this topic can be pursued further, one must go back to the principle of spirituality that Christ Jesus had illustrated with the parable of the Samaritan. It must be acknowledged that there are a lot of people in leading positions who do not walk by on the other side, but aim to help the injured traveller who can be seen to represent humanity.

Let us consider, for example, the efforts of the top man of the U.S. Federal Reserve system, who falls into this category, who devotes all his efforts to keeping price inflation as low as possible in order to protect the value of the nation's money. He does this by regulating the money supply and imposing interest rates in such a manner as to keep the physical economy at a state of constant semi-starvation. If nobody has any money, then, the value of money remains high, so the reasoning goes.

Except, it must be said that this reasoning is faulty. Experience has shown that such an approach destroys the productive sector so that much fewer goods are produced than were produced before, which then become increasingly expensive, as everyone may have noticed in recent years. Historic experience has shown that the effective price to earnings ratio has always been at its lowest in an environment of bountiful production aided by high technology processes.

Now the question must be asked, how does all this tie into Christ Jesus' parable that illustrates the nature of spirituality?

The answer to the puzzle lies in the wording that Christ Jesus had used. He tells us in the parable that the Samaritan pours oil and wine into the wounds of the injured. How does this compare with the process the Federal Reserve is pursuing, which is centered on semistarvation? It doesn't compare very well, does it?

The Federal Reserve process is analogous to a man who sees the wounded man by the wayside and kneels down at his side with a knife in hand to deepen the wounds already inflicted in order that other people passing by by may find it easier to steal, if at all the initial robbers had left anything behind. There is no spirituality at the root of a process that is centered on manipulating pain as a factor to enrich society. Still, this is the chosen process of today. The elite's financial riches are protected by the society's deprivation, imposing austerity and life destroying conservatism. Such an approach is fascist in nature. It takes away the foundation for civilization and for the supporting structures for human life.

It is true that semistarvation has kept humanity at a static population level for nearly 800,000 years before human intelligence began to unfold. However, at this equilibrium the world population remained steady at an extremely low level, near the one million mark. This tiny world-population was all that the natural system could sustain. Today's vastly larger civilization, in contrast, is sustained primarily by advanced technologies and high density energy production. Right now, the foundation for this energy and technology structure is oil. But oil is a finite resource. Soon the oil fields will become dry holes, so that evermore exotic and expensive technologies will be required to squeeze the last drops out of them. And, then, what? Without vast new developments in nuclear technologies, the needed bountiful inexpensive energy production cannot be achieved. As a consequence, today's population pyramid that rests totally on an energy and technology foundation must collapse, and civilization must regress to a kind of technological state and population level that corresponds to that of the dark ages.

The problem with the Federal Reserve austerity process is that it is centered on a built in deep, deep, artificial poverty which cannot support the needed scientific, technological, and infrastructural development on which human life has become to depend. The privately operated Federal Reserve process, must therefore be regarded as a very deadly process, which it is. The advance guard of today should therefore demand the complete removal of this deadly process that is represented not only by the Federal Reserve and similar institutions, but also by the IMF and other similar global organizations. Unless this call is made, and Lyndon LaRouche is making this call, and the call is heeded, which it isn't, mankind renders itself unfit to survive. The truth of this statement is actually already being felt in many parts of the world.

Lyndon LaRouche proposes to take the Federal Reserve out of the hands of private speculators who play the games of the Empire, and make it a federal bank, which, then, enables the nation to replace the deadly financial processes that the Federal Reserve is pursuing and supporting today, with a process designed for infinite development. By nationalizing the Federal Reserve the nation would issue itself interest free credits for its self-development. This type of process is very much in line with the process that Christ Jesus has defined as pouring in "oil and wine" into the wounds of the injured man, in order to heal them.

Lyndon LaRouche sees the model for such a federal institution in the federally owned Bank structure that was created on the principle of the nation-state and was first set up by Alexander Hamilton in the early years of the United States of America. Hamilton's federal bank was a development oriented banking structure in which created credits were transformed into creative physical processes that reflected themselves as wealth for the nation. Today, Lyndon LaRouche's call for the re-establishment of such a system is, unfortunately, answered with disdain. The world wants its feudal interest payments, and it wants twice, or twenty times, the the amount that the productive economy earns in profit. The world calls LaRouche an extremist because he insists that the physical economy cannot give away what has not been produced. He is an extremist, indeed, in that he attacks the modern society's belief that it can make up the shortfall between what it needs or demands and what it produces by stealing from each other, beginning at the poorest of the poor.

The scientific fact is that Lyndon LaRouche doesn't go far enough. Mankind's survival depends on the little realized fact that it must first rescue itself out of the mental trap that supports the present system of poverty which involves conservatism and stealing. Mankind needs to rebuilt the mental infrastructure that existed at the high point of its last period of renaissance, the kind of infrastructure that had enabled the creation of a vast range of technologies and industries, including the technology for practical scientific Christ healing that had flourished for a while under the name of Christian Science.

---

# Chapter 8 - Spirituality with Lyndon LaRouche

When Lyndon LaRouche calls for convening a New Bretton Woods conference, he is looking for a world-wide agreement on the setting of fixed international exchange rates in order to create a stable financial platform that is essential for long term development. Such a world-wide agreement is necessary for shutting down the current orgy in international currency speculation that is destroying the value of national currencies. The New Bretton Woods system that he speaks of also includes the nationalization of the U.S. Federal Reserve by which the nation's money supply would be put back into the hands of the nation. Without these two moves, Lyndon LaRouche warns, no meaningful development of any kind can take place on this planet, or a stable currency be established.

The two aspects, stability and development, are really a single unit. Neither aspect can exist in isolation. There is no stability without development, nor development without stability. The existence of such interrelationships had been recognized over a hundred years ago in a different context, by Mary Baker Eddy. Lyndon LaRouche has recognized the same phenomenon in the economic and political arena. Nothing can be repaired on the international economic scene until the money supply of at least the world's largest economic block is taken out of the hands of the financial manipulators and speculators. Whatever is build on imperial ideology and processes cannot be made a foundation for stability, no matter how hard one may wish this, as the imperial mode of operation is designed to create instability for easy exploitation, and to destabilize nations by which the Empire gains control over them.

If the two steps outlined in LaRouche's New Bretton Woods proposal cannot be accomplished, the presently collapsing world-financial system will continue to collapse until it disintegrates. A system that has become self-destructive cannot be saved unless its nature is changed. However, if the two essential steps for stability and development can be achieved, a new environment becomes established in which the steam-rolling train of disaster can be derailed that has wreaked havoc in the world since the Specie Resumption Act was passed in the U.S. in the late 1800s. In this case a whole new era of stability and productivity will be ushered in.

Currently, the speculators steal from each other as they trade illusions for money while passing the same financial instruments to each other at ever higher prices until the game stops. In this process of trading nothing is ever produced while the valuations keep rising and the nation's investment resources are drained from the productive economy into the mythological sphere of the easy money treadmill. Only when the counterproductive processes become shut down, will the society find the funds again, and the incentive, to pursue productive processes with which to enrich itself. This type of direct investment into the realization of the society's productive potential, can be seen as analogous to the pouring in of "oil and wine" into the wounds of society's needs.

LaRouche specific call for a New Bretton Woods type conference was apparently not issued because the previous Bretton Woods system had offered an ideal solution, which it did not. This system had lacked many essential elements by which it was doomed to fail from the outset. Rather, the call for a New Bretton Woods conference was issued, because the bankers and politicians around the world know what this type of system represents in a broad sense, how it basically should have worked, which sets the stage for a useful starting point. Nor would any convened New Bretton Woods conference likely go far enough, even if it includes the nationalization of the U.S. Federal Reserve, because in order to provide complete stability in the financial world the entire oligarchic system needs to be shut down that drives the speculative binge today, as well as the entire U.N. dictatorship apparatus that represents and supports the oligarchic structures, both of which have deeply injured humanity.

It is evidently impossible for development oriented processes to succeed while injury is being inflicted behind the scene.

Lyndon LaRouche, therefore, has set his aim at eliminating the British Empire in its entirety that not only creates havoc on the financial scene, but also supports the international drug trade, and finances, safeguards, and logistically supports virtually every terrorist organization in the world, which it employs for the destabilization of nations. Lyndon LaRouche has long advocated that entire oligarchic apparatus must be shut down for the security of humanity and the its urgent need to develop itself in order that it may utilize its potential and exist in an environment of peace. Christ Jesus' parable of the Samaritan can not find its reflection on the political scene without a commitment by humanity to shut down injurious processes and power structures, wherever they exist, rather than shutting down the future of humanity with injuries on a vast scale as the imperial power structures demand in order to perpetuate their existence.

In this pursuit Lyndon LaRouche aims at the Empire's ideological front, its antipopulation ideologies that call for the removal of between two and five billion people from the face of the planet. He aims at shutting down the IMF which is presently the strong arm dictator of the Empire's starvation policy which carries out the imperial demands for economic austerity and environmental dictates which are presently murdering close to 100 million people per year throughout the world. This is what Lyndon LaRouche aims to bring to an end. The oligarchy cannot be expected to shut itself down, or to change its game.

If mankind is to have a future, it must hope that Lyndon LaRouche succeeds, and support his efforts. Except, none of this is likely to happen without a strong revival of the society's spirituality, reflected in its motives and acts. This is its power. The imperial oligarch, as reflected by its actions and demands, is evidently totally devoid of even a trace of spirituality. Its goals for humanity have become increasingly more fascist in nature and murderous in deed. History presents an unbroken record of imperial fascism from the days of its slave trade and dope operations, right to the modern day financial looting operations and its taking control of the world's food supply on a near global scale.

That imperialism has no foundation in spirituality is evident by the vast separation of the imperial treatment of humanity, from that which Christ Jesus has outlined as the natural manifest of spirituality.

Seen from a scientific standpoint, the extremism that Lyndon LaRouche is accused of by the imperial press in its vicious slander, is actually too conservative in comparison to what is really required. The question, therefore is not whether Lyndon LaRouche will succeed in having his policy proposals adopted, the real question is whether mankind will have the strength to rescue itself from its impending doom by pursuing the foundational changes that are necessary, of the type that Lyndon LaRouche merely hints at. The apparent extremity of his proposals, that some people view with horror, indicate to some degree the fast distance that mankind must move in order to assure its survival on this planet and achieve continuing growth, which are really one and the same in essence.

Mary Baker evidently understood the explicit nature of the spirituality that Christ Jesus has illustrated in the parable of the Samaritan, and projects this onto her discovery. She writes, "Christian Science is not a dweller apart in royal solitude; it is not a law of matter, nor a transcendentalism that heals only the sick. This Science is a law of divine Mind, a persuasive animus, an unerring impetus, an ever-present help."*6

That this type of Christian Science has been carried with her to the grave is self-evident. But the demand of the spirit that it represented cannot be buried. The same spirit that had reflected itself in what Mary Baker Eddy understood is beginning to unfold anew in the lives of modern pioneers, such as Lyndon LaRouche who has evidently rediscovered the spirit of spirituality in his own way, though he never actually uses the word to define himself. None the less, his efforts reflect to an astonishing degree the nature of spirituality as it had been illustrated by Christ Jesus in the parable of the Samaritan.

In Science, spirituality is understood as a native component of the nature of the human being. This component can evidently be silenced, as it has been all too often. It can also be developed to unfold as the pioneers illustrate. One thing, however, cannot be said about it, namely that it depends on religious or intellectual backgrounds, or is a political, national, or partisan thing. It is universal and can unfold in the whole of humanity. It unfolds from the infinite source that is reflected in every human being who is sensitive enough to recognize it. The best of these are the great pioneers of humanity.

Indeed, the world has brought forth many scientific thinkers and pioneers whose advanced discoveries have fundamentally altered the social scene, who have established an environment in which an entire society was able to prosper. Perhaps, these pioneers didn't define the root of their advances as resting on spirituality, but it was.

Nicolas of Cusa was one of those pioneers. He had helped lay the foundation for the Renaissance. He was a genius inn many ways, but was most deeply involved with spiritual matters, and had worked to apply the resulting discoveries for the advancement of society. Gottfried Wilhelm Leibnitz was another such man, who understood the potential of mankind's grand intellect. He was one of the chief contributors to the spirit of the American Revolution. Alexander Hamilton, in turn, created a political financial environment that brought prosperity to an entire nation, and for an entire century to come.

Whichever pioneer stands at the forefront of the world's scene today, continuing this trend, does not need to be another Cusa, Leibnitz, Hamilton, or Mary Baker Eddy. Their work is done. The need in today's world it to go forward. Today's pioneer is clearly one who builds on the legacy of the past and projects it into the future.

This type of pioneer is most exemplified by Lyndon LaRouche.

During the last 30 years, Lyndon LaRouche has devoted his life to efforts to change the world into a world one would be proud to live in. He had seen the poverty of colonialism when serving oversees during World War II, and in later years he became concerned with his own country's policies that supported the imperial feudal structures and was undermining the strength of his own society. Thus, in association with a few friends, a movement was born that now exists in virtually every country. One must acknowledge that his efforts have met with remarkable success in may areas, which is the natural hallmark for all human efforts founded in spirituality. Of course the success of his efforts are rarely acknowledged in the world press that loves slander better than truth - much of which was focused on Lyndon LaRouche. And when slander didn't achieve much, active persecution began. While he survived attempts at assassination, he couldn't avoid being incarcerated for 5 years under a grotesque political persecution that has begun to back-fire and may soon unravel the entire corrupt criminal justice system.

If Christ Jesus were to formulate his parable about the Samaritan in today's world, he would have to present the Samaritan as a pioneer working under the most treacherous circumstances. He would have to show him being shot at, maligned, slandered, railroaded into prison, and he would have to show him as continuing his work from the prison cell for the advance of the global society. London LaRouche was treated in this manner. Mary Baker Eddy was treated in a similar manner, only much less harshly so. Christ Jesus was nailed to the cross in a political effort to silence his voice. The opponents of human development feel themselves so utterly impotent in the arena of truth that they must meet their opponents with the sword.

Many of the pioneers for human development have been executed by the ruling Empire's throughout the ages in an attempt to halt their influence and darken the riches of the spirit they represented. All the American presidents that were assassinated in U.S. history, were assassinated for fundamentally this same reason. Their names are all well known, from Abraham Lincoln to John Fitzgerald Kennedy, each of which was strongly involved in national and international economic development. Alexander Hamilton, who laid the policy foundation for the early internal development, was murdered soon thereafter. He was shot in a duel, into which he had been manipulated in the defense of honor. The only U.S. president who was strongly dedicated to the advance of national and international economic development, who was not assassinated in office, was Franklin Delanor Roosevelt. Strangely, however, he died

of natural causes, virtually at the very moment that his usefulness for saving the Empire from Hitler's attack had ended. Joseph Stalin never believed the story that his death was unaided. He was convinced that Franklin Delanor Roosevelt had been murdered in a clever way: "They poisoned him," he insisted, "as they have tried to poison me!... The Churchill gang!"*7

While it cannot be said that Lyndon LaRouche ever cleansed a leper or cured enteritis, as did Mary Baker Eddy out of the depth of her spiritual strength, Lyndon LaRouche did make far reaching contributions to the advance of mankind's spiritual infrastructure by which such healing can be achieved again on a universal platform. In this wider arena, progress is indeed most urgently needed. Mary Baker Eddy knew that her Science was too faintly understood, so that a hidden structure would be needed for the redevelopment of the scientific principles that she understood, and that this structure would have to come to light through the process of discovery itself. It was to be a science for the unfolding of spirituality in human consciousness.

The need for scientific progress in understanding fundamental principles has never been greater than it is today. Still this need is not fulfilled by duplicating the achievements of the past, even to the point of duplicating Mary Baker Eddy's work. The principle of progress requires that mankind move beyond even the tallest achievements of the past. Whatever has been discovered and demonstrated in the past, doesn't have to be discovered again. It just needs to be applied. Nor can one stop here. The call is for an evermore advanced awareness of the truth about the infinite nature of the human being, and this at the grass roots level of society where such movement is absolutely essential.

The essential task of today is far greater than just to heal a leper and to cure enteritis. All these are well within the capacity of mankind's present technological understanding. The challenge of today is to shift the entire healing process onto a higher level in order to secure the foundation for life, itself, which is constantly being eroded.

The shift in focus that is needed to secure the physical platform through intelligent processes of development, doesn't make the process any less spiritual because the object is to enrich the physical world. Isn't this what Christ Jesus had done when he healed the lepers and raised the dead? He raised the physical environment by mental means, and he raised the self-perception of mankind up with it. The object of the Christ process was to improve the physical manifest, in order to cause it to reflect the quality of the spiritual idea that the corporeal organization represents.

The same process must necessarily apply to the state-organizations of nations. Its physical sphere must reflect the quality of the spiritual idea that is imbedded into the identity of mankind as the manifest image of God, the reflection of the higher power or reality that may be termed God or fundamental Principle.

The evidence in physical manifest of an unfolding spiritual idea can be found almost daily, and everywhere, when one looks closely, even though the connection between the evidence and its cause is commonly denied. All the essential elements that support human existence, such as food, housing, transportation, industrial production, rest on a foundation that is made up of principles and ideas without which the society can no longer physically exist. Therefore, by implication, mankind's existence on this planet has a profoundly spiritual foundation. This foundation is not a mind over matter dominion where mankind is at war with the natural universe, to subdue it. Mankind's dominion on this planet is not a dominion over the natural realm, but is creative dominion over limitations that reflects mankind's spiritual capacity for infinite creativity which lawfully enhances and enriches not only the human realm, but also the natural world.

The natural world is actually at risk in an environment of human poverty. Much ado is made over the world's disappearing forests, for which the advance of civilization is blamed. The opposite is the case. The lamented destruction reflects the effect of a growing global poverty. The vast majority of the forests that are cut, are still cut for firewood, or to make way for primitive agriculture that yields very few returns. Some researchers believe that these two causes, all by themselves, account for 90% of the global forest destruction. In a highly advanced society, the need for this type of destruction no longer exists. Who needs fire wood when nuclear energy provides the human need for energy in an infinitely cleaner and more abundant fashion? Likewise, who needs to toil the primitive life in burnt out jungles when advanced agriculture can provide a hundred times greater yields than primitive processes ever will?

The outcome of creativity provides the physical resources that are essential to life. These created resources simply do not exist on any other platform, except on this naturally spiritual and intelligent platform. This is the platform that Lyndon LaRouche has endeavored to raise, that he has devoted his life to.

Lyndon LaRouche calls himself an economist. This may not be an accurate definition, because the same term also applies to other economists who see great virtue in poverty and therefore aim to trim the human race back to those more primitive levels by means of starvation,

increased diseases, and the countless effects of underdevelopment which these false 'economists' like to impose upon targeted populations. Justice requires one to set the record right between economists who build upon spirituality as a basis, and the poverty oriented economists who aim to built upon injury a new centrally dominated world order in which no one is free. It requires one to make clear the existing night and day separation between an economist devoted to injury bound economics centered on poverty and depopulation, and an economist who is devoted to the development of the infinite potential of the human being. The factor that highlights this separation is spirituality.

It should be noted that spirituality is not religion, although some religions are designed to awaken the native spirituality of man. For thirteen centuries after the era of Christ Jesus' demonstrations of mankind's spiritual dominion, spirituality became smothered almost to death in Europe. The most monumental advance in civilization that had occurred up this point, identified today as the Greek Classical era, had been literally erased the unfolding imperial disregard of spirituality.

The Greek civilization began with a literal miracle, by which a primitive mountain culture had raised itself within a few short centuries into the most advanced culture on the planet. It brought forth geniuses like Solon, Socrates, Plato, Eratosthenes, and Christ Jesus who emerged at the tail end of that era, and with a tie to a long standing monotheist culture. Still, none of this unfolding spirituality had been able to stand against the Roman Empire. Greece lost 87% of its population under Roman control. This is how the dark ages begun, that would have been exceedingly bright ones had mankind learned to acknowledge and cherish its spiritual strength.

The so-called Christian church that rose out of the ashes of that renaissance, never became a spiritual institution. It fulfilled various functions within the structures of empires. In fact, the church itself, held back the spirit of discovery and creative reasoning for many ages. The church became known for its inquisitions, which had nothing to do with any search for the truth. It became the center of brutality and torture. It became a tool for controlling the masses and keeping them in the dark. It had no room for creative reasoning of the type that had flourished before, and was still flourishing in China at the time of the dark ages in Europe, bringing there a rich harvest in advanced discoveries.

China had made tremendous cultural and technological advances while Europe had kept itself tied into knots in its dark ages.

Both of these developments, somehow, ended in

the 14th century. The long chain of cultural advancement in China had ended slightly earlier when the Mongol hordes ravished that land. The great darkness that had gripped Europe had at last made its way into China from where it returned with a vengeance in the form of the Black Plaque. But then, at the end of the 14th century a renewal of spirituality began to take hold in Europe that quickly mushroomed into what became the Renaissance. It must be said, therefore, that the beginning of 15th century marks the real turning point in European history that the Christian era of the first century should have been, and might have been if the Roman Empire had never been born.

The reference point in time that marks the first century AD did not become the marker for a new era of advanced civilization such as the Renaissance represented later, merely marked a bright spot on the horizon of time that was quickly snuffed out and remained so for 15 centuries. In real terms it marks the beginning of an ugly and long drawn out succession of dark ages filled with wars and pestilence and slavery of which the Black Death plaque was merely one of the more dramatic examples. This marker in time which marks the first century AD may also be regarded as that point in time at which the European society's cultural development had become suspended. The advent of the Christ era that the Christian world celebrates was in real terms held in abeyance and did not really begin to unfold until the 15th century when true spirituality was reintroduced on a universal scale.

Spirituality is the term that identifies the conscious recognition of the divine spark of reason that makes the human being special compared to any other species on the planet. It was this spirit that was exemplified by the Renaissance and was exemplified earlier by Christ Jesus where it had its brightest manifest. The term, renaissance, therefore, was chosen to acknowledge the renewal. This it what the term means. This is what has occurred in the 15th century in Europe. The spiritual driver for civilization, that had been buried in Europe for over thirteen centuries, had suddenly been rediscovered with such a profound understanding that it caused a literal rebirth of the society on a foundation of spirituality.

Spirituality created the Renaissance in as much as it had powered the confucianist ideology that had given China the world's most advanced culture at a time when the European society was mired in poverty, toil, disease, and war. Spirituality is also the prime determinant that distinguishes one school of economics, that which embraces poverty, underdevelopment, and depopulation (which is an imperial invention), from its opposite school of economics that embraces mankind's potential for infinite development. Lyndon LaRouche is an economist of the school of this second type of infinite economy. This school is squarely rooted in the principles that were brought to light during mankind's periods of renaissance.

In a very real sense, Lyndon LaRouche promotes the rediscovery of man's spirituality, although he never says so. He promotes the discovery of the principles that were brought to light most profoundly during periods of renaissance and sets them up as examples of what had once supported the greatest advance in civilization.

Another identifier of spirituality is its universality. The Golden Renaissance of the 15th century was not specifically a Catholic renaissance, or even a Christian renaissance, although the Christ idea was prominent in the foreground, nor was it a Muslim renewal. It was a universal humanist renewal. A super-denominational spirituality unfolded that embraced the whole of society in an elevated self-perception. The same principle is promoted again by Lyndon LaRouche. It has become as a foundation for his work in economics, because both aspects unfold towards infinity. In fact, one cannot exist without the other. True spirituality cannot exist without a corresponding manifest in economic development. The two cannot be isolated from each other. Either one has them both, or one has none. In this sense, Lyndon LaRouche may be one of the few proponents of true spirituality on the planet, today, especially so in economic and financial matters.

The problem with religious zeal (that the society mistakenly terms spirituality) is its isolationist nature. Religious zeal is built on myths and is focused on esoteric aspects which close the door on the fundamental principles for meeting the human needs of society. Mary Baker Eddy defined it as "blind enthusiasm" and "mortal will." Christ Jesus illustrated the nature of narrow zeal in his parable of the Samaritan by the priest who saw the injured man lying at the side of a road, but walked by on the other side, but who made strong demands on society to obey customs, rites, and festivals. Such enthusiasts as he give little regard to uplifting humanity. Spirituality is always blocked by self-serving ideologies. Spirituality can never be self-serving. Months before Lyndon LaRouche's publications were shut down and he was railroaded into prison he had been warned and given a chance to renounce his stand on the issues in defense of humanity. He refused. The Samaritan binds up the injured man's wounds and puts him on his beast. As Christ Jesus told the parable, spirituality creates a rich human scene in which all parties are elevated. The world has greatly benefited since, then, from the result of his refusal to renounce himself.

His very first speech after he was released from incarceration, contained an exploration of the metal development processes that led to the emergence of the Golden Renaissance. There was no looking back. The need was to go forward. Nor has he stopped since. He warned about the collapse of the world-financial system and its impending disintegration, and presented proposals for an orderly renewal. This speech was given before countless billions had evaporated when many a huge financial institution collapsed and nations were poverty bound to the point that death by starvation became evermore common in many of the nations in which the IMF imposed brutal austerity in order to shore up its dying system.

It appears that 50% of LaRouche's efforts are directed at exploring the underlying principles of civilization, and the other 50% are devoted to exposing the processes that violate these principles. In conjunction with this, he proposes specific policy applications of the underlying principles in order that they may not be violated but utilized. His hopes are that the world's social scene may become founded on the vital principles that both, support mankind's existence, and raise the status of its civilization.

History has shown that poverty economics involve a lack of spirituality, a lack of vision, a lack of creative reasoning, a lack of scientific enquiry. In some instances this lack is created artificially in order to hide the invariable fact that poverty results as a consequence of looting. Today's poverty economics include both aspects. Physical poverty, and mental poverty. The two are rarely found in isolation. They are aspects of a single phenomenon. Physical poverty reflects an underlying mental poverty, and both reflect axioms built on mythologies, such as the mythologies that underlie the present world-financial system in which financial aggregates are deemed wealth as they pile up into the stratosphere, while at the same time the physical economy which they should represent, is collapsing at an ever accelerating rate.

In today's world the ever increasing separation of the physical sphere (which is collapsing) from the financial sphere (which has become a bubble of fantasies) is being kept carefully hidden beneath a cloak of imperial mythologies that embrace no valid principle, but hail looting as a legitimate process for creating wealth even though nothing is produced by the process in real terms, except chaos and destruction. The created mythologies hide the fact that looting (the modern form of is called speculation) destroys the productive economy, which the financial aggregates stand as a claim against. Thus, the separation between reality and fantasy is growing larger and larger by the day towards the day of equalization when the reality hits home that there is nothing there.

In the scientific sense, mythology and spirituality are opposites. The Greek poet Homer appears to have understood this. His poetic works, the Illiad and the Odesy, were structured in a manner as to expose the irrational nature of the mythologies that had controlled the lives of the primitive mountain tribes of his nation. Homer is rightly regarded to have laid the foundation for that early renaissance that historians call the Greek Classical Period. Lyndon LaRouche has embarked on the same type of quest, namely to expose the vastly more dangerous mythologies that prevent mankind's natural self-development in the present period. His goal is, to reverse the foundation of the mythologies (especially economic and political mythologies) with spirituality, in a quest for an understanding of what is actually real in fundamental terms, and to save the world from it's impossible fantasies that generate not wealth, but decay.

The sad part is that mankind likes to look back into its history for entertainment, without projecting the past into the future as a means for determining the ideal present course, which comes to light as advanced development. The churches have prayed for two millennia for the reappearance of Christ Jesus, without ever recognizing that this reappearance has in fact occurred in many forms by which human civilization has been elevated beyond measure. Civilization has grown by means of developments of advanced spiritual understanding. The evidence of that, which we see today, is found in events that brought the greatest renewal of human dignity of all times, known as the Golden Renaissance, and in such documents as the Constitution of the United States of America that reflect the spiritual attainments of the advance guard of this development. On this advance guard stood tall pioneers, some of which are well known, and some are not. Lyndon LaRouche is clearly one of them.

In a sense Lyndon LaRouche can be regarded as a spiritual pioneer, to the extend that he promotes an understanding of the higher power on which human existence is founded and is reflected in mankind's state of civilization to whatever degree this is recognized, understood, and applied. Mary Baker Eddy was one of the great spiritual pioneers of an earlier century. One of her leading edge contribution is found in her defining the higher power, commonly called God, as divine Principle, Mind, Soul, Spirit, Life, Truth, and Love. This is also the arena where one finds Lyndon LaRouche most active, because it is in this area where the healing of humanity is most urgently required needed if the greatest catastrophe in history is to be avoided. This is in this arena were mankind has been most severely robbed and injured, and left to die. This is the arena of spirituality in which the human spirit has been defeated which is evident by the utter tragedies that have become common place.

In order to stop the utter tragedies, this defeat must be turned into a victory that uplifts the whole of the human scene.

The leprosy of today is mental. It is evidenced in the enslavement of children for monetary profits that has engulfed 250 million kids into anything ranging from military use to sex slavery, to sweatshop labor for pennies an hour. The mental leprosy of today is also evident in the millions of land mines that have been laid the world over, that are claiming countless lives daily. It is also evidenced in those richly financed mercenary warfare games for imperial objectives, that are unleashing genocide in many places, especially in Africa where the toll has far superseded that imposed by Adolf Hitler. It also evident in the economic murdering of up to 100 million people each year by means of starvation and underdevelopment related causes. It is evident in the growing emphasis on "right to die" legislations, which stands against the background of 33,000 children under the age of 5 being denied the right to live. They are being denied the right to exist as the means for their living has become decimated under the present world-monetary system that has become increasingly hollow and self-destructive.

The mental leprosy of today is evident in such insanities as mankind's self-denial that is reflected in the termination of advanced energy development on which its future depends. It is evident in the growing destruction of the world's health-care infrastructures in the face of the greatest potential biological threat that a severely weakened population base represents. It is evident in a world-economic ideology that has amassed immense wealth for a few, but has destroyed in the process the livelihood of many of the great nations of the world. Germany, for instance, the once greatest economic powerhouse on the planet, has become the leader in unemployment. Russia is in a virtual state of anarchy, ruled by organized crime for international looting. Even the Ukraine, the bread basket of the world, finds its population at the edge of starvation.

London LaRouche has devoted his life to the healing of this mental leprosy. For this he went back into the history pages of mankind's greatest humanist achievements, for the discovery of fundamental principles with which to counter the ideological mythologies that rule the axioms of today. He speaks of the human being as created in the image of God. Except, to him, these are not idle words reflecting empty theological phrases. He sees a reality that has substance. He sees a reality in which man unfolds as the grand creator by virtue of an intellect that has no equal in the entire known universe.

Mankind's spiritual understanding is grounded in demonstrated accomplishments of the highest order, that have put today's society on the pinnacle of all that manifests life. This is the foundation from which Lyndon LaRouche works in the pursuit of political policies for the advanced development of humanity. This also sets his efforts apart from entropic ideologies that reach from a self-appointed zenith down to poor humanity with dictatorial demands. His efforts are none-entropic in nature as they begin with a grounding in demonstrated achievements and become a projection that open the scene to infinity. The hallmark of spirituality is none-entropic development that embraces the infinite as man's native sphere. Lyndon LaRouche sees a potential in humanity that is greater than himself, and is greater than the highest achievements in all the ages. He has literally touched the fringes of infinity and beckons mankind to follow. Here spirituality and politics meet.

---

# Chapter 9 - The "son of a year" Concept"

The following, in regard to exploring the spiritual dimension of leadership. In this regards I disagree with Lyndon LaRouche that man is created in the image of God, because man is much more than that.

In ancient Hebrew a month was called "son of a year." If man is seen in this context a whole new 'quality' for humanity comes to light. No longer is humanity perceived as an external appendage that bears the image of God. Instead, man is perceived as a constituent part of the Infinite, or God.

If man is seen as an external appendage made in the image of God, we open the door to 'spiritual' Dawinism, rather than to the infinite capacities that are forever ours to express.

This phase change in perception that reverses false notions that have existed for centuries can have far reaching implications in the political sphere in regard to leadership in the world, and more importantly, in regard to how this leadership is acknowledged. We have everything in place today that is needed to save humanity from a great catastrophe as its global financial system disintegrates, including a brilliant leadership. But there is little acknowledgment of that leadership, especially not where this acknowledgment should most naturally be found. All this has something to do with the self-identification of humanity. Allow me to present a brief visualization.

Create in your mind a four-element square matrix. This matrix has four rows and four columns of elements. Let us perceive the four rows as four levels or domains of thinking, and label these from top to bottom as,

1. The Word,
2. The Christ,
3. Christianity,
4. The trials of Christianity.

The columns then represent four distinct areas of development. But the rows are most important for the problem at hand.

The three lower rows, evidently represent the three great domains in which humanity unfolds. This renders the upper one someone detached and remote.

The separation leaves us the lower structure of the three domains to work with. Common logic tells us that this lower structure can be effectively split in half, since Christianity has been historically divided. Indeed, the face of humanity has been soiled with blood and gore, and bears the marks of all the atrocities of many dark ages. Christianity is also rich with enormous advances, scientific and humanist developments, and so forth. This duality produces a divided structure, which turns the lower system of three rows into a confrontational structure.

Functionally, there is a big difference between conflict and confrontation. For instance, it is common knowledge that 12 million children under the age of 5 are put to death each year by humanity, as surely as if they would be shot, for the simple reason that humanity refuses to provide the necessary care in terms of readily available treatments, clean water, safe shelter, sufficient food, and so forth. Now, most people agree that this large scale economic murdering creates a terrible situation, but they feel impotent to do anything about it. This puts them into a conflict with themselves, with their sense of good, with their sense of humanity, because they are stuck here, they can't take the problem further to a resolution. They see a paradox that they can't, but which they refuse to resolve. This is a conflict.

Most of humanity is trapped in this sphere of conflicts they feel impotent to resolve. These conflicts occur at almost every level of society. Only the oligarchy, Prince Philip and the like, appear to operate on a still lower level, because this trap does not conflict with their goals. They regard the needless death of 12 million children not as a tragedy, but as a fulfillment of a part of their depopulation objective. Nevertheless, the end result is the same. They are trapped just the same by their mindless objective, which prevents them from developing a real solution in which no one has to die. So it is that each year 12 million children are needlessly sacrificed. The reason is not that nobody cares, but that there is no leadership to break the deadlock.

A confrontation is needed to break the deadlock. A confrontation is needed to resolve the conflicts. This confrontation involves the entire confrontational structure that we created out of the lower three rows of the matrix, divided into two halves. In the upper half, human development involves the recognition of mankind's strength and the spiritual ideas that have become the hallmark of man in terms of creative discoveries. These ideas that are developed in the upper half, transform the lower half by means confrontation. The lower half corresponds to humanity's problems, its conflicts, its self-confinement, its assumed impotence. The confrontation involves the use of science and discovered principles. These widen the scope of perception, which enables the creation of technologies and productive processes and so forth. By this uplifting confrontation the lower row becomes effectively redefined to represent the Science driver of Christianity by which the problems or systems that generate conflict are eliminated.

Today, humanity as a whole appears to be trapped at this very low level of self-confinement, which corresponds to the lowest row of the confrontational matrix, but there is no active link to the upper half. Strangely, nobody seems to mind this. Perhaps this is so, because humanity has lived in this arena of perpetual conflict for more than a century, and has deemed it to be normal. The entire speculative world-financial system is built on a foundation of conflict. This is even regarded as desirable, and healthy, and a lot of people believe this to be true. Thus, nobody minds the conflicts, even if the whole thing is about to blow up and take humanity with it. The fact is, most people defend this insane system of gambling on a galactic scale by which society steals from itself and calls this profit.

There exists a near homogenous thinking throughout the wide field of humanity, which reflects all the characteristic of the lowest level of self-confinement. This may be the reason why any real leadership, like that of a Lyndon LaRouche, appears disturbingly revolutionary. The reason is, that this leadership reflects a quality of thought that is foreign to those who are thinking at this level. They regard everything that exists outside their scope of thinking, that they cannot comprehend, much less deal with, as revolutionary and unrealistic. This creates a challenge for leadership. If they talk about leadership, this means to them that someone, somewhere, has taken the initiative to move certain things around within the confines of their level. If the world-financial system bleeds, patch it up; if it disintegrates, apply crisis management. This is what leadership means to those at the lowest level where conception is self-confined by certain barriers which have been largely artificially imposed.

This is the reason why nothing positive is achieved at this level, why endless cycles of crisis and crisis management follow each other in a spiral of doom. In real terms, the concept of leadership at this level is not an aspect of leadership at all. It is a false sense of leadership that is designed to strengthen the mental trap for maintaining conflict. All this is far from being normal.

One finds a beautiful example of the normal interplay of leadership and humanity presented in the Noah story. This story has its history in the distant past of the twin river valley of the Tigris and Euphrates rivers. We find the occurrence of huge floods recorded for this region in Akkadian scripts. But this arena was also one of ever changing types of empires and interaction between people, so that the spiritual development that was wrought in this period would naturally be included in the legends of the times. Now, with all this considered, I would like to focus on one tiny aspect in the Noah legend that is remarkable for what it portrays and for what it tells us about the author of the story. For one thing, this tiny episode hints at a high level of understanding by those early people, the kind of which is largely absent within the homogenous thinking of modern society. Furthermore, within this context, the legend also illustrates the nature of true leadership.

The specific episode is centered on Noah's sons, Ham, Shem, and Japheth, and the son of Ham, called Canaan. We are told that Noah was found naked one day, and drunken, in his tent. Ham found him there. Apparently with great excitement Ham rushed about and told everybody. Shem and Japheth responded by taking up a garment between them and going backwards over their father to cover their father's nakedness.

When Noah found out what was done, he announced: "Cursed be Canaan; a servant of servants shall be unto his brethren."

Now, what justice is there in this, in the denunciation of Canaan, who was not even involved in the affair? The comment makes Noah look like a most cruel man. Ah, but was it really a denunciation? Did Noah not rather confront the entire pornographic environment that the son of Ham was growing up in, which would render him a servant of servants if it was not altered? It would trap him into an homogenous thinking with his father's mentality. The fact is Noah is portrayed as the only person in that story who is concerned about the child.

Noah blessed the God of Shem, and added that "God shall enlarge Japheth, and he shall dwell in the tent's of Shem."

The nature of leadership.

We have two types of leadership indicated in this part of the Noah legend. One is the leadership of Japheth. As Noah pointed out, Japheth shall dwell in the tents of Shem. This is to say that what Japheth represents invariably finds a natural response in the hearts of humanity. In this example the leader and humanity are essentially on the same level though they reflect different types of development and frames of interest. In other words, this type of leadership exists within the context of horizontal diversity, when represented on a matrix.

Now, Noah reemphasized that Canaan would be their servant. Evidently, the isolation of the domain in which this leadership was effective, was recognized to be a problem, even then. Nothing was mentioned that the conflict that Canaan was trapped in, would be resolved.

Now we need to ask, was the role of Noah cast as that of a leader? In a way it was, but his was a different type of leadership. Noah's role was cast to introduce a higher point of reference into the equation. Without his comments the story would have been largely meaningless. Except, Noah's point of reference, apparently, was based in the absolute domain which lies outside the confrontational structure, by which the confrontational structure becomes superseded, and a reflective structure describes the higher process. This is the inevitable result when on takes the confrontation to the n'th degree, that is, if one explores the universe to solve a paradox or conflict. In this case one comes upon the Christ idea and the infinite reality that it represents. By this, one's point of reference is shifted to a higher domain and the entire human scene is put onto a different platform. One of these higher points of reference is the perception that man is the Son of God in the same context that a month is identified in Hebrew texts as "the son of a year."

Can this break the deadlock of isolation that puts mankind's true leadership outside the normal sphere of reference? Perhaps is can. We can explore this by considering how a dead poet once defeated Napoleon.

Friedrich Schiller was a leader of the type of leadership that was ascribed to Noah. His point of reference was evidently founded in the reflective structure that includes the absolute elements that are not a part of the confrontational structure. Schiller, however, operated with both structures simultaneously. He understood mankind's conflicts and encouraged the people to confront those conflicts in their own thinking, and to do this on a specific scientific platform that presents humanity with an extremely high dignity and worth. In other words, he created a new image for humanity that all could aspire to and reflect in their own private lives. By this pioneering effort he recreated this higher point of reference in the minds of those of humanity whom he was in contact with. He worked with the confrontational structure, but even as he did, he introduced the reflective structure of reality. Thus, he could speak with authority about the confrontational domains, and do this in a manner that did not isolate his leadership because his points of reference were now understood by the people of his time. By these means his leadership continued even after he was dead, because his points of reference had become also the people's points of reference on all things.

It is being said that Franklin Delanor Roosevelt was a great leader, because he pulled a nation out of its deepest depression and turned it into the richest nation on the planet, and he did this even while a war was fought at the same time. But was he really a leader, because of this? It seems he merely reactivated the principles of economy that Hamilton and Lincoln had discovered before him, and utilized them to the utmost degree. Indeed, he would have applied these principles to uplift the whole world, and he would have been successful had he lived past the end of the war to fulfill his dream. He had the power to do all this, and the trust of the population. But was he a great leader because of this? No! He was merely a wise man and a great administrator, occupying a powerful office. The fact is, when he died, everything that he created, that he had fought for, that he had hoped to achieve, was overturned within weeks at the hands of traitors. This would not have been possible in an environment of prior leadership, for then, the principles that he understood and fought for, would have been universally understood and would have motivated the whole of society by which they would have been protected. Had F. D. Roosevelt been a great leader, mankind's understanding of the principles that he understood would have been strong and would have carried the day and fulfilled his dream long past the day of his death, as this was the case with Friedrich Schiller.

Napoleon's mentality, of course was so low that he never even reached above the level of self-confinement to conflict's that had trapped a large part of humanity. Napoleon's thinking would have blended well with the homogenous thinking of today's humanity; with its fascination with various types of pornography, including political pornography; with its 'information' age pornography, and the 'pornography' of financial transparency that demands a nation to undress itself in public in order that its weakness can be intimately examined by the speculators. It is certainly true that the information age hype is pornographic in nature and destroys the freedom that comes with creative discoveries and scientific processes.

Schiller was quite aware of the information pornography trap. He encouraged people to elevate themselves by discovering their nature and capacities; to ennoble themselves through the development of their spiritual resources. To confront Napoleon, intellectually, with this higher leadership would have achieved nothing, yet he was defeated by it. We have the same situation today. It appears just as impossible, today, to inspire the world's would be leaders to set up a new Bretton Woods monetary and economic system to replace the one that is now disintegrating. Still, it is also certain that this meeting will take place, with or without them.

Passing on information is not the issue. The issue is creative discovery, which can only be shared by recreating the basis for creative discovery everywhere in the world.

Ludwig van Wolzogen could have told Napoleon that his Russian campaign would destroy him. Wolzogen knew this before the first soldier ever set foot on Russian soil. He understood this from his knowledge of physical economy that he had learned while being associated with Schiller. This doesn't sound like much of a basis to fight a war on, but it was the decisive factor. Wolzogen's sensitivity to the dimension of physical economy evolved out of his sensitivity to humanity, its needs, and the productive processes by which these needs are met. Napoleon's needs were great. He had an army of 435,000 men to feed and to supply, daily, with 300,000 horses which required fodder every single day. Wolzogen also understood that Napoleon's processes for meeting those needs were unnatural and unsustainable, as they were based on stealing and looting, which is in economic terms, insanity.

Wolzogen could have told this to Napoleon again when he stood at the gates of Moscow with his remnant of 90,000 troops, but Napoleon would not have seen the logic for his defeat and would not have surrendered. Napoleon was a brilliant man is some respects, but he was brilliantly insane, and he was leading the insane. He had lost close to 500,000 men during the march to Moscow (including reinforcements). Still, he was still hoping to succeed.

The important factor for his defeat was the result of Schiller's leadership. Although Schiller had been dead at the time (Schiller had been assassinated some time before) his spirit of humanity was still very much alive in the hearts of many. It had shaped their own leadership. Of course, Napoleon was not familiar with Schiller's higher point of reference, but the War Commander of Moscow evidently was, who ordered the city's evacuation so that it could be destroyed. The destruction of Moscow by Russia's own hands was crucial for defeating Napoleon. Wolzogen was leading the Russian defense, and had become a real leader in his own right. It was evidently Wolzogen who stood behind the Russian perception that physical property, even that which was the pride of the nation, was of little value compared to the lives of the people and the sovereignty of the nation. Thus, the sacrifice was readily made in order to protect that which must never be sacrificed.

The kind of response to leadership that we see here, reflected Schiller's values, even though Schiller had been dead. We must achieve the same level of leadership, and the same level of penetration. I think we can do this by bringing a still higher concept of man into the human equation that sets up a new point of reference for humanity. Here, the "son of a year" concept becomes important, which tells us that in as much a month is perceived as son of a year, so humanity can find its place as a constituent part of the infinite whole of reality, rather than being attached to it.

I believe this is what Lyndon LaRouche represents, or should represent, and the two structures that are involved with effective leadership - one to be elevated and obsoleted, and the other to be brought to light - offers a useful platform for rousing humanity to the level of thought at which LaRouche's leadership can be affective. Lyndon LaRouche is not an isolated leader. His knowledge and ideals have become the knowledge and ideals of many, whom he had uplifted out of the homogenous background of conflict oriented self-confinement. No real gap stands between his leadership and the homogenous conflict oriented thinking of humanity, therefore, there is hope for humanity. There is hope for humanity, because his pioneering discoveries and processes for discoveries are now leading the way within the consciousness of those who have replicated his discoveries and made them their own discoveries, rather than being ruled through authoritative dictates. Through LaRouche's kind of leadership the collapsing world-financial system can be replaced before it disintegrates, if society reflects his leadership sufficiently through its own internal thought processes. In this case humanity will not go down with the sinking Titanic, because it will not allow itself to do so.

If this kind of leadership transparency cannot be established universally, God help humanity, for then its lot is as hopeless as Napoleon's was when he held out for a month in that burnt city of Moscow that had become a hell hole of stinking ashes, senseless looting, murder, and massive drunkenness. When Napoleon finally ordered the army to move out, soldiers could be seen carrying useless loot in great quantities. They loaded up the few horses that were still alive, with furniture and jewelry, none of which had any value to them on their return treks through the icy dessert of Russia in winter. Napoleon was insane, leading the insane. The insanity was so great that 70,000 men were lost to the cold of the winter, and to other causes, during the first 150 miles of their march back home. This march took nearly two weeks.

A similar thing can be said about today's world-financial leadership. It is not surprising that Lyndon LaRouche's leadership role is not acknowledged in the halls of financial institutions, because what he represents is true leadership that goes beyond the speculator's scope of vision. Obviously, there is a resistance being generated against his leadership, as his leadership would defeat the oligarchic world system. Still, the fact remains that if the thinking of humanity can be ennobled with a higher identity for mankind, this force can ignite the same kind of processes of discovery and self-discovery that Schiller had inspired people to pursue.

Sure, if someone had suggested to Napoleon that he capitulate when standing in front of the gates of Moscow, that person would have been shot for treason. Nevertheless, had this person had been successful the lives of 100,000 people would have been spared and a great city would not have been destroyed. If this could have been achieved Napoleon would have made the first right decision in his entire life. Now one must ask, is such a feat impossible to accomplish, even though it never occurred throughout history? The logical demand upon this age is, that this be done.

For this, one needs to focus on the poverty that reigns within domains of conflict. Then one needs to confront this poverty with the riches of humanity. Some of these riches can be found within the long forgotten structure of the seven days of creation. If this story is seen as a historical narrative, nothing but confusion results. If, on the other hand, this story is regarded as a platform statement that defines the awakening of humanity to its place in the sun as the Sons of God, in as much as a month is called "the son of year", we have a dynamism available for discoveries about our role in the universe that may just pull enough people out the general homogeny to inspire a landslide of change.

The creation story, as an account of creation, must be seen as mythology. However, the author of that story may have merely utilized the core frame of the ancient creations myths that came out the time of the Old Classical period under the rule of Hammurabi, and used this frame to convey an awareness of what really defines man, such as letting in the light, dividing the light, etc. etc.. The story culminates in defining man as being made in the image of God, followed by rest or an acknowledgment of completeness. This may have been the highest concept available in the ancient world and represents extremely advanced thinking for this time. Nevertheless, the story is flawed. It is no longer recognizable as accurate, nor is it sufficient to meet the needs of our time. It is, in fact, a bearer of a trace element of mythology.

Before the Greek Classical period began, there was a poet, Homer, who had dealt a death blow to Greek mythology, and on the strength of this had elevated human values. His leadership, which gripped and inspired his nation as it offered a resolution to the mythology, saved that nation. Before the phase change that he created, the Greek nation (such as it was) was on much the same level that humanity is at, today, confined to poverty by the power of its mythologies.

Today's mythologies are called financial transparency, free-trade, bubble economy, postindustrialism, environmental terrorism, information pornography, political pornography, and so on. The modern Gods may no longer be called Zeuz, but they hold humanity into a tight confinement where conflicts can be recognized, but can never be resolved.

If humanity is to survive, it must find its true value against which all else pales, like Russia had done when it defeated Napoleon. Except this task is not achieved by one's saying that it must be so. The reality about ourselves must be explored. This is where the two structures come into play again. They were first perceived as a platform for exploration more than a hundred years ago.

They were perceived at the high point of the last great renaissance on the American shores which came out of the background of Hamilton and Lincoln. The structures were created by a scientific explorer of Christianity, who became known world wide under the name, Mary Baker Eddy. She had outlined these structures in her work, but left them open to be built out of humanity's own resources. They provide no answers, but open the scene to a lot of questions to which answers must be found.

As a part of this outline she provided a Glossary of building blocks that consists of 144 definitions, enough to provide a nine part superstructure for each of the 16 elements of the foursquare matrix. Some of these are parts of dual definitions. Mary Baker Eddy presents five distinct types of dual definitions as a foundation for recognizing their existence elsewhere. For one type the duality is vertically separated on the matrix, for another the separation is horizontal, and then there are types of duality's where no separation is possible. There are five types altogether, the most remarkable type is that for the term, son, which has its own point of reference added, which superimposes upon the definition of son the concept "son of a year."

The metaphor for these five types is incorporated into the design of a crown that represents the factor 5, but which also in the same design represents the dimension of 9, 16, and 144. The symbolism that she created includes a reference to both structures, and the structures themselves have been specifically designed to precisely accommodate the platform of the seven days of creation. She then placed the symbol of her crown, together with another symbol, on the front cover of every book she has authored, in the form of a seal. This seal represents the scientific processes of self-discovery that she had been dealing with, possibly in the hope that someone, at some point in time, would through the process of discovery, rediscover these structures for scientific and spiritual development that she had been dealing with.

As of this writing, this structure remains largely unknown. Nor is there any interest in wanting to know. The world, apparently, has not changed much. There was no one at her time who could remotely comprehend the depth of the processes that she had considered. This was the time the when Eugenics theory had been conjured up by the Malthus, Darwin, and Galton 'team' of the British Empire. This theory of evolution and Eugenics presented a damming image for the value of man that, by means of extensive information pornography, became immensely popular and had opened the gates to two world wars. This information pornography became a weapon to destroy the deep reaching leadership that Abraham Lincoln had established, which had lived on for a long time in the hearts and minds of the nation after Lincoln had died.

It may be that the time has come for a new pioneer's work to bear fruit, finally. One item of this work appears to be immediately useful for its higher point of reference, the "son of a year" concept, to counter all lower perceptions. Mary Baker Eddy had superimposed this concept upon her dual definition of son, pertaining to the contrasting duality of the "Son of God, the Messiah or Christ," versus the "son of man, the offspring of the flesh." The higher aspect of this duality, actually represents a still higher dimension of perception, which was presented in Volume 6a as Mary Baker Eddy's fourth dimension, of Spirit. As was pointed out in Volume 6a, Christ Jesus covered all four dimensions in his work. Unless these are recognized, his work remains shrouded in mystery, but when they are recognized, his leadership once again becomes effective in the world as the principles that he understood, become understood again to carry the day.

Mary Baker Eddy was a similar type of leader than Christ Jesus. And like it was with Jesus, her leadership was far in advance of her day. Her leadership needs yet to be established, fully, and this can't happen until the principles and perceptions that are interwoven into the fabric of her structure for scientific development, described in this book series, enables human consciousness to elevate itself by its own resources. Thus, mankind becomes its own leadership based on its discovery of fundamental principles that may even supersede at some point what Mary Baker Eddy understood about her work.

Through this awakening a facet of leadership may be brought to light that might yet be able to stir up the sleepy homogeny of mankind's low level thinking and self-confinement into conflicts, and create a permanent breakout condition for the self-advancement of humanity, and its permanent self-leadership that comes to light as a natural discipline to absolute principles.

_____

# Chapter 10 - What is the future for mankind in terms of advancing its spirituality?

The sky is the limit! There has never existed a greater opportunity for mankind to assert its right for dominion, than exists now. We are at the threshold of a historic opportunity for mankind to liberate itself from the processes that have defaced its image, undermined its existence, bound it mentally into a tight confinement more impregnable than any prison house. The opportunity that mankind has at this hour is greater than any opportunity it had in history. The systems are falling apart that have devastated mankind for ages. At the same time great infrastructures for spiritual development have been brought to light and have been implemented in many respects. This heightens the chance to realize the potential at hand. Except the opportunity must be met with a strong spiritual resolve, or else it, too, will become lost like many bright opportunities in the past have become lost, when in such cases the great moments met a small people, as Schiller had put it. In the scientific context, small means that a person is self-confined into a sphere of conflicts that either are not recognized, or if recognized, are not confronted.

If the opportunity that mankind has at hand at this moment, to free itself from oligarchic confinement, is lost, the ensuing tragedy is beyond contemplation, nor would anything productive be achieved by visualizing it. What needs to be visualized instead, and realized indeed, is the kind of deep reaching agitation that terminates the prevailing insanity which tolerates lies at its very core of thinking with which it endangers civilization today.

The real target that a society's leadership, or self-leadership, must address itself to, that it must destroy as surely as Ludwig von Wolzogen new that Napoleon had to be destroyed for any nation to be save in Europe, is not the might of the presently ruling empire; or the craftiness of its oligarchy; or even the brutality of its fascism. Not a single advanced leader who ever walked the earth succeeded at such an attempt. The target in every successful campaign has always been to raise the conscience of humanity; to agitate the hell out of it; to confront its errors, its false believes, its defective axioms, and its apathy. When all this is achieved, everything else that is needed for victory falls into place. The goal in liberating humanity must be to annihilate the homogenous insanity that keeps the bulk of humanity tied to the ground and confined to self-destruction.

# Chapter 11 - The Dynamics in Responding to Leadership.

There exist three structures in which a society can find leadership, that it must respond to, by which it can rise up and improve itself until that moment occurs when it is prepared to take a quantum jump, or paradigm shift in thinking, to the next higher level of leadership. The leadership is not personal, in such cases, but is provided by the successive structures for scientific and spiritual development. The leadership that these structures provide reflects the demands of absolute principles, rather than arbitrary personal demands.

The three structures in which humanity can find leadership, correspond to the four dimensions of spiritual perception that were touched upon in Volume 6a, the highest of which is the forth dimension, of Spirit, where man comes to light as the "Son of God, the Messiah, or Christ" as Mary Baker Eddy had put it. The lowest dimension is the sphere of self-confinement and conflicts that is devoid of leadership. It is a sphere of insanity by which society destroys itself as it had done so in past ages.

The world is presently approaching this stage at which its self-destruction may occur in spite of all ongoing unfolding of true leadership. This self-destruction occurs whenever the existing leadership fails to reach the critical momentum. This self-destructive, self-confined state of existence reflects the current state of society in many parts of the world. In today's world countless human beings are readily sacrificed for profits that have no meaning, by which the survival of nations is disregarded for the higher priority of saving the currently dying world-financial system. By this madness the very continuity of life on this planet is put in doubt as the physical structures that support human life are being destroyed while humanity is facing the strain of the still existing (and newly deployed) nuclear weapons that are controlled by the same insane elements that have already demonstrated their willingness to sacrifice entire nations to protect the systems by which they are looting the world.

This type of insanity produces a dismal state of affairs, indeed. It appears therefore (mistakenly so) that one might define a still lower form of existence on the scale of spirituality. It appears that a lower state could be defined which represents fascism and dictatorial oligarchism, both of which have murdered humanity in huge numbers for centuries. Except this notion is wrong, and most deadly so.

It is deadly, because it creates a false target. The battle cry should be, don't fight the despot-kings, fight the insanity that allows the despot-kings to rule. The only valid target that one may aim at, that one must defeat, is the homogenous insanity that already includes in its sphere all the elements of destruction that are presently tolerated, such as oligarchism, fascism, globalism, etc., which represent a void of spirituality, or insanity in a scientific sense. The fact is, there is no lower state possible than that which has been presently attained by large segments of society, at which society becomes self-destructive. Society cannot sink lower than that. This state, at which no spirituality is reflected, is an absolute state, as absolute as darkness. Such a state has no definable structure by which redemption could occur. Still, it is not beyond the reach of the leadership that naturally unfolds in the three higher dimensions. This open door is the salvation of the world.

# Chapter 12 - Three Types of Leadership

One needs to recognize that insanity has a great density. Advanced leadership may be too far out of reach to be effective, while the domain of insanity is invariably a "hell" of various types of conflict. This means that some precisely structured type of leadership is required that addresses the specific issues to cause an interruption, or a revolution, that upsets the hellish processes. If the interruption or revolution cannot be achieved, the society invariably destroys itself by its insanity, as it undermines the foundation for its existence. Alighieri Dante was evidently aware of this when he created his three part epic poem that explored "Hell", "Purgatory," and the scientific "Paradiso."

One possible exit that lets society escape its default fate, is the kind of revolution where entire nations are turned upside down. Revolutions occur when the conditions resulting from insanity become intolerable and a somewhat less insane leadership exists that exploits the brooding ferment for its violent reactions. In this case the corrupt institutions do become replaced, but rarely does such revolutionary leadership uplift the state of civilization. To the contrary, revolutionary convulsion becomes ultimately more destructive, because revolutions do not raise the quality of thinking to such levels that a more advanced state of civilization results. They tend to regress into violent power plays in which life becomes cheap and murder the rule of the day.

Unfortunately, in an environment of conflict there is no mental 'movement' occurring that could give rise to creative discoveries of such structures by which a redeeming process could be initiated or implemented. This means, that within this containment to a zero state of existence, an advancing type of leadership is essential, such as we have today to some degree. The rescuing moves begin when the confinement is removed.

Lyndon LaRouche's leadership in forecasting the impending disintegration of the world-financial system is an example of the kind of leadership that has the potential to break the mental confinement of humanity. He is known throughout the world as a political activist who confronted the self-confinement of humanity into a sphere of insanity and conflict.

In its confinement society may be compared to a herd of lemming racing towards the proverbial cliff. LaRouche's leadership is such that it must convey the danger and the reason for it. Thus, he puts up stop signs, warning of the nearby cliff and its danger. Unfortunately, only a few take heed. The rest race on. But his leadership is also impeded. The oligarchy of the world runs after him and plugs up the signs he erected, saying to the lemming "we don't want you to stop running; we want you to die." Thus LaRouche is chided by the lemming themselves, for his constant warnings. But he is not deterred. He says that he will keep up the warning for as long as there is a breath in him, even if the last sign must be put up at the very edge of cliff. And he does more. He tells the lemming that they must not only stop, but turn around and rebuild their economies that they are running away from, that they must redevelop their infrastructures for living. The real lemming, of course, won't be able to do this, but humanity has this ability.

Indeed, some of LaRouche's warning is heeded. China is redeveloping itself in the most massive way imaginable. Its water development project centered on the Three Gorges Dam, has the potential to open up new areas for agriculture of the size of Germany, with which to feed its expanding population and help feed the population of the world. China's greatest commitment to human development, however, is a plan that LaRouche had urged long ago, which he called the Eurasian Land Bridge Development project, that would interconnect Europe and all of Asia with a development corridor of rail lines, communication lines, power lines, water mains, and oil distribution systems, and more. China is now fully committed to making this project a reality, which promises to be the biggest development project in human history. But the oligarchy says, NO, and urges its lemming to stay on their suicide course. It has made it clear time and time again that it does not want humanity to live. It wants humanity reduced to 10% of the present population, which it believes would create the most ideal environment for its feudalist based empire to flourish.

China, however, continues its course. LaRouche's leadership now finds a reflection in China's own leadership. By this progress step of self-developed leadership, China has become a main target of the oligarchy's war against human development. Within months after the Eurasian Land Bridge Development Project was announced, the oligarchy destroyed the economies of the leading Asian nations that would play a key role in this vast continental development. Unrestrained globalism enables the destruction of nations by financial manipulation, to be accomplished with ease and for rich profits. Still, China's commitment to the Eurasian Land Bridge development project is stronger than ever, with more and more nations now joining the commitment. It appears that only nuclear war can stop the final realization of this age old dream of linking all nations of the largest continent of the earth in a comprehensive self-development effort. The war to stop this appears to be in preparation right now. Recent developments have made it quite clear that the faintest excuse based on fraudulent reports, will suffice to launch this war. That is how the bombing of Iraq was launched, even while the U.N. nations were debating the issue. And together with China, Russia is targeted for its daring to isolate itself from the IMF and its policies for looting.

Is the world doomed, therefore? No it isn't! And this is where the structure for leadership comes in. While the most insane cannot be redeemed, it is possible nevertheless for the insanities to be confronted with reality. LaRouche does this. His scientific dissertations agitate the waters with undeniable truths, and the effect is that the homogenous nature in mankind's thinking disappears. Some people do begin to think, and they add to the agitation and the confrontations that expose falsehoods. By this process a political mass movement has been born. It has been born out the scientific necessity that the prevailing insanity must be confronted; that it must be confronted to such a degree that it weakens it, or destroys it altogether. This confrontation causes cultural paradigm shifts in the right direction. The end result is, that the quality of thinking is raised to such levels that a new civilization may be born. When this happens a renaissance unfolds in which the oligarchic structures have no place to exist.

When this happens humanity has entered a new sphere. It won't be a sphere of ease and painless bliss, however. It will remain a sphere of healthy confrontations in which all limits that would tie man to the dirt of the earth are confronted and overcome. In this awakened sphere is life and movement. Therefore, such a sphere has a definite structure.

Whenever a conflicting state is being addressed sufficiently to break the bondage, the confrontational structure that maps out the principles for freedom becomes activated.

All this means, that there is no lower structure below the confrontational structure. Anything lower is a dimension-less zero that has no structure at all. The zero-dimension state has no principle or truth in support of it. It exists outside the realm of the reality in which man's true image is defined.

When the zero state and its confinement in conflicts is torn apart by confrontation and spiritual sense once again determines the course of humanity, the advanced leadership becomes the leading edge of

mankind and a vital component of stable progress. In some cases the activation of the confrontational structure occurs when the destructive processes that act upon humanity become so absurd, and the insanity so gross, that the dormant spiritual sense of humanity can no longer be confined. Often, the breakout conditions that "wake" humanity out of its slumber are incurred by the fascism of its oligarchy that reigns supreme in the sphere of homogenous insanity. The Golden Renaissance, for instance, was built almost directly on the ashes that humanity was reduced to, after the world-financial system of the time disintegrated in 1345 under the pressure of unsustainable looting. The fact that half the population of Europe perished at this time seems to have been a sufficient wake up call to start the confrontation of the destructive evils in earnest.

By this awakening the oligarchy was dealt with as was needed, but think how much death and destruction could have been avoided if the financial insanity of the time had been successfully confronted before it took the house down. This is the danger that Dante had labored to expose by raising the quality of thinking throughout the whole land. He may not have been aware of the depth of the destruction that would ensue, and that it would take 100 years for Europe to recover from the consequences. Nevertheless, after the recovery had rebuild much of what was destroyed, Dante's work did eventually help ignite that great renaissance that occurred a century after his death. Who, therefore, can tell, today, where humanity would stand were it not for this single man's devotion to the cause of providing leadership?

On fundamentals such as these rests the hope of mankind, because the break-out conditions that have once changed and uplifted the world in the past can be recreated. Nothing else offers any hope. These conditions have to be recreated if this present civilization is to survive. Today, there is a movement in this direction, almost becoming a flood. Mankind's spirituality, although it is rarely recognized as such, is reasserting itself. It has been nurtured in the background for many decades.

Lyndon LaRouche's assessment is, that the breakout point was reached in October 1997 when the dying world-financial system began to fracture. This ended the status quo. The world entered what he described as a boundary layer between either total disintegration into a new dark age, or a total renewal and the beginning of the greatest renaissance ever. In this boundary layer the reassertion of spirituality will be the deciding factor, and the changes will be swift and enormous in scope.

A financial analyst once told this author that the

breakdown of even the smallest of Canada's five major banks would be an inconceivable disaster for the nation. One can measure from this comment the enormous scope of a comprehensive global disintegration, and this not only of the banking systems world-wide, but of the entire global financial system.

Lyndon LaRouche insists that mankind cannot allow this to happen, and he predicts that we will witness in this boundary layer rapidly occurring world-shaping events of ever greater magnitude. He writes: "Beginning approximately October 1997, the world entered a critical boundary-layer of current world history, a presently ongoing process of abrupt, radical changes in opinion and institutions, after which almost nothing will be the same as prior to the time this tumultuous boundary-layer was first entered. Vast amounts of nominal financial holdings will be simply wiped out, including the great majority of nominal financial assets on the books today. Many governments and leading political parties will be swept away, their wreckage left, like mangled ruins rotting on the beaches, after one of the greatest storms of this century. Much of what had been leading opinion, too, will be swept away, or exist only as dusty, quaint curiosities among little-noticed records. The adducible rules of political life are now undergoing an accelerating rate of change, into a new direction. It is unlikely, that any way of acting which was deemed successful prior to the entry to this boundary layer, will succeed during the developments now unfolding."*8

Some of this has already occurred. The world has seen changes that would have been deemed impossible before, such as the reorientation of Russia, Malaysia, Japan, China, the bombing of Iraq followed by the nuclear rearmament of Russia. We have also seen the Empire's desperate attacks on the American President escalated to absurd proportions, only to fail time and time again. We have also seen the repeated traps the Empire has set for the man, became dismal failures that created a backlash. There is a great wind sweeping the scene. There are deep reaching movements in progress. Virtually everything is being challenged and confronted with references to truth, even while the lies are barely hatched. But there is also the development of nuclear war on the horizon that can erupt as quickly and for no apparent reasons, like the Blair and Gore instigated bombing of Iraq had demonstrated.

There existed no reason for the bombing of Iraq, and the pretext was a fraudulent report that virtually everybody knew was a fraud. The real target, however, was far greater than anything connected with Iraq whose citizens were slaughtered as a target of convenience. This bombing was intended to change the world, which it did. It demonstrated that any nation who stands against

the Empire, like Russia now does which refuses to be looted any further, can be targeted at any moment for the flimsiest excuse and be destroyed. This is the calling card of the would be U.S. President, Al Gore, and his British instigator, Tony Blair.

Like Iraq, Russia lacks the resources to repulse a massive attack, but it does have nuclear waepons. The Empire seems to hope that Russia with use them. In fact it seeks this as a pretext to finally unleash its long cherished plan for destroying the world and most people in it as it had talked about for many decades already.

Right now we are in a boundary condition. This Empire's planned fate for humanity may yet be averted. The destruction of President Clinton, which brings Al Gore to power, is a key element that will decide the future of humanity. The coup d'etat against President Clinton is the same as that which brought Adolf Hitler to power, and is instigated by the same people for the same expected result. Still, mankind has not been defeated just yet.

When the Titanic entered the ice field its boundary condition began where its course and speed became critical, but its destruction could have been avoided. Only when the great ship collided with the iceberg that ripped a 200 foot gash into its hull was the Titanic put beyond the point of no return, and with it, the majority of its passengers. The ship could not be saved form this point on, by any means.

For the present world-financial system this point of no return has long been crossed. The world-financial ship is done for. It can no longer be saved by any means. But for humanity, the point of no return has not yet been reached. It won't be reached until the first missiles are launched for the destruction of Russia, or China, or Iran, India, Iraq, the Sudan, or the U.S.A.. The boundary condition terminates only at this point, or at the point when the controlling powers are eliminated that would have those missiles launched to further for their goals.

LaRouche says that this confrontation does not have to be drawn out to the last moment where it may coincide with the disintegration of the world-financial system. None of this has to happen. The world-financial system can be taken out of the hands of its present controllers and be put through an equitable bankruptcy reorganization. Thus, humanity can be protected as the dying system is put to sleep before it disintegrates. President Clinton, too, can be protected and be exonerated, and Al Gore can be removed from the White House. The USA can even join China as an active partner in the Eurasian Land Bridge Development Project. LaRouche can be called into the White House to launch the USA's own national and continent wide redevelopment projects. The USA can further commit itself to build a land link to Eurasia via a 50 km tunnel cut through the bed-rock beneath the Bering Strait.

Mary Baker Eddy assures humanity that it has no need to lay itself down to die in a senseless, murderous conflict. There are alternatives to conflict. LaRouche has stated long ago that these alternatives are boundless economic development that create a golden age for all, based on the spiritual resource of mankind, its creative discoveries, and their application.

Indeed, what more does humanity need beside its spirituality that can never be extinguished, with which it is able to transform the world according to fundamental Principle that no one can mock with human will nor escape from in order to evade its effect? Thus, the survival of humanity rests with itself, and the current developments provide more than just a faint hope for a bright and prosperous future, because the same 'grain of Truth' that assures mankind's survival also open's its horizon to infinity. This makes the long sought goal of mankind's boundless self-development achievable.

# Book Complete - THE END

# About the research series:
## *Discovering Infinity*

The series is made up of nine books , created by Rolf A. F. Witzsche, in North Vancouver, Canada, over a span of more than 15 years.

Work on the series began in the early 1980s, but its central element is rooted in a new form of science that had been created a hundred years earlier by a New England woman named Mary Baker Eddy (1821-1910). The woman was probably the most accomplished scientists in the field of exploring the power of intelligent perception for elevating human existence. The science became widely known for its application for the healing of disease on a scientific metaphysical basis. While the series presented here focuses on the leading-edge aspects of her science that are still largely unknown in today's world, the series takes us still farther back in time, to the work of another great pioneer of humanity, to Dante Alighieri (1265-1321) who is regarded by some as the first stepping stone towards the Golden Renaissance, a period of scientific and spiritual development that uplifted mankind probably more profoundly than any other period in history. A new self-perception of mankind dawned that ended the Dark Ages and uplifted the world. Both developments stand tall among the great turning points in the history of mankind.

It is sadly obvious that we need such a renaissance-turning-point again in our modern dark world. Our world has become a world of unspeakable fascism, greed, war, terror, torture, inhumanity, nuclear bombs, slavery, poverty, and financial disintegration. I addition to that we face the return of the Ice Age that's looming darkly on the not so distant horizon. With these shadows fast falling around us we find that our civilization hangs in the balance once again, and more precariously so than it did in the time of Dante who foresaw society's doom and worked to prevent it. As in Dante's time the strength of our civilization is failing; our defences are wearing thin; our riches are crumbling; and the light of our hope for getting out of this trap is getting small, matching the smallness in thinking that has become the hallmark of modern society.

Dante found himself in a similar kind of world. His home city had been the center of the greatest financial world empire up to this time, which was rotten to the core. Dante became a rebel bearing warnings and presenting critical choices that could have avoided the doom that later happened. But instead of being heeded Dante was banished from the city.

As a rebel in 'exile' Dante poured the principles that he understood into his writings. The best known of these works is his epic poetic trilogy the **Commedia,** or translated, the **Divine Comedy.** The **Commedia** is a serious work designed to lift society out of its 'smallness' by raising its perception of truth and its self-perception to higher levels of thinking. The **Commedia** presents three such levels, presented in a progressive sequence. Dante's three levels are incorporated into the makeup of the research series presented here, which is focused on our modern world.

In order to be able to do accomplish the complex task that Dante had laid out for himself, he had to first create a high-level language, a new kind of language with a depth and quality that can convey the complex ideas that he wanted to express. On this track he gathered together the most beautiful aspects of all the Italian dialects that he could find from the numerous sources across the country. It is being said that he literally created the Italian language for this purpose. Of course there was nothing more worthy of that language than his own poetic works. The language that he created became the central language of the Golden Renaissance, the Italian Renaissance, the renaissance typified by the Council of Florence of the mid 1400s. Dante would have been proud of this development, but he died long before the Renaissance became a reality. Nevertheless he understood the principles that the Golden Renaissance represented, and he expressed these principles in the **Commedia.**

The **Commedia** tells us the story of a pilgrim and his guide. The two journey together through the three stages that Dante called: **Hell; Purgatory; and Paradise.** The research series presented here is designed to follow this three-step pattern. In fact, it is designed to take us through the journey twice, once in the perspective of the pilgrim, and once in the perspective of the guide. For this reason the series is made up of six sets of books, Volume 1 through 6.

Volume 1 through 3 are written from the standpoint of the pilgrim.

**Volume 1** corresponds with Dante's concept of **Hell,** but seen in modern terms. Actually Dante's personal hell has been two-fold. He was a rebel against the financial empire of his time. He saw doom spelled in big letters in the corrupting decadence that stank with arrogance but was in real terms a hollow, empty shell. He must have spoken out powerfully with calls for sanity for which he was banished from his beloved home city.

While he didn't live long enough to see the collapse of the financial system that he had warned about, he understood that the system would collapse by the sheer weight of its gravity if it continued its course, and by the weakness of its emptiness. The collapse occurred 24 years after Dante's death, with consequences far worse that he might have imagined. The collapse had weakened the population across Europe so severely that it opened the door to the Black Plaque that swept like wildfire across the land and destroyed nearly half the European population.

Since we are now poised for a replay with a possibly deeper and wider financial collapse, the first book of the series, Volume 1 (Volume 1A) focuses on the hell that Dante had fought against. The tile for this volume is, **The Disintegration of the World's Financial System.** Indeed, when the mighty giant that is deemed as solid as the Rock of Gibraltar becomes an empty shell the inevitable happens.

But Dante's personal hell had a second feature, that of injustice, inhumanity, death threats; he was banished under the threat of death. The modern face of this feature becomes the focus for the second part of Volume 1 (Volume 1B). It focuses on the crimes committed by those who would uphold today's dying private empire in order to hold back its built-in demise. The tile for this volume is, **Crimes Against Humanity.**

In the Greek legend in which Saturn is devouring his sons, the god-giant perpetrates this crime not in a rage of 'greed' so that he may nourish himself, but out of fear. Dante the poet had been banished by the mightiest financial empire of his time, out of fear. The empire had been scared of the humanity of the poet.

**Volume 2** mirrors Dante's concept of **Purgatory,** a stage of healing. The title for this volume is **Science and Spiritual Healing.** The healing here is a kind of self-discovery, the discovery of a spiritual dimension in our humanity that takes us beyond the crude limits that we have placed on ourselves in the 'smallness' of today's prevailing closed-minded thinking.

**Volume 3** takes us to still higher ground. It presents the scientific platform of Christ Science, Dante's **Paradise,** but advanced in great measures to a true science. At this stage the pilgrim finds that the guide inevitably leaves him standing alone in order that he may be guided by his own human resources. America's spiritual pioneer, Mary Baker Eddy, the founder of Christian Science, the discoverer of "the divine Principle of scientific mental healing," has done exactly the same. In the late 1800s she developed a vast pedagogical structure for scientific and spiritual development, evidently in support of her science, but she left humanity

alone with it. She only outlined its design, even though the structure is so enormous in scope that it encompasses all of her major words, with some strikingly advanced concepts added. She never imposed it as a dogma as to how it must unfold in the mind of the student. Just as the guide stepped aside at this point in Dante's poem, Mary Baker Eddy had posed a lot of questions in the way her pedagogical structure is outlined, but she never really provides any answers for them. It is as if she is saying, like Dante had, that the answers must emerge through the process of discovery as one individually begins to search for the truth.

**Volume 3** presents the details of the discovery of Mary Baker Eddy's pedagogical structure and the subsequent exploration of it. What is presented in this volume resulted from a process in which one is always alone, supported only by the substance of science and the spiritual riches of our humanity. The title of this volume is: **Universal Divine Science - Spiritual Pedagogicals.**

At this point the second cycle begins. The next three volumes, Volume 4 through 6 take us through the same journey once more, from Dante's **Hell,** to **Purgatory,** and to **Paradise,** but from the standpoint of the guide instead of the pilgrim.

**Volume 4** takes us through **Hell** as seen by the guide who must plot a safe path through the jungle. Here the great concepts demand clarity: Is evil a power, or is it a negation without power? Is darkness substantial, or is there substance only in light against which darkness cannot stand? The title of this volume is, **Light Piercing the Heart of Darkness.**

**Volume 5** explores the dimension of **Purgatory** with the eyes of a guide who must turn the spiritual potential, by means of science, into a profound renaissance that uplifts the whole world. In this case the guide understands the advanced pedagogical structures that the pioneer of the past has provided, who then finds himself challenged to apply them to create a portal to a new world. The title of this volume is, **Scientific Government and Self-Government.**

Perhaps the profoundest realization that we have learned in the historic periods of renaissance is the now evident fact that our 'bread' does not come from the sky, from heaven, nor does it come from the Earth, but is created as the product of the human mind, drawn from the discovery and application of universal principles in which our infinite dimension comes to light.

**Volume 6** is once more split into two parts, both representing Dante's **Paradise** from the standpoint of the guide. The first part, Volume 6a, has the title, **The**

**Infinite Nature of Man.** Mary Baker Eddy made a statement in 1884 that must have shaken the starched motions of that time. She wrote, "Woman is the highest term for man." In the context of her science this statement bears not a sexual reference, but a spiritual one. It reflects the highest concept of humanity that we find described in the biblical Apocalypse as "a woman clothed with the sun and the moon under her feet and on her head a crown of twelve stars."

This non-sexual reference to woman as a metaphor for the spiritual identity of mankind, the highest idea of our humanity, comes with no small challenges attached for one to live up to. It is no small challenge to discover what worlds upon worlds it encompasses. In this realm even the guide is alone, and infinity itself becomes the frontier where there are no inherent limits.

The second part of Volume 6, (Volume 6b), is focused on the spiritual dimension of leadership. The title for this final book in the series is simply called, **Leadership.**

So what is it that we are after to provide leadership for? What kind of leadership makes any sense in the infinite domain? Is the goal to achieve victory? Or does a new type of leadership unfold that raises the standard of achievement?

The research series presented here contains still one more volume, the **Introduction Volume** that opens the series. Its title is, **Roots in Universal History.**

This introductory volume sets the stage for the series by exploring who and what we are as human beings in the vast scope of universal history. In this sphere of the real world the roles of the pilgrim and the guide are blurred and intermingle. In this sphere we are all but children growing up, or children that refuse to grow out of their infancy as it is so often the case. In this sphere history sometimes offers itself as a guide, but to what end? And who listens anyway what history tells us? Dante must have felt that society needs more than just history, because history by itself comes with an empty promise all too often. Dante must have felt that something more is needed, like timeless principles and a humanity with built-in riches that we have barely begun to explore, much less to utilize. Evidently Dante wrote the **Commedia** to open the door to this universe of principles and the wide dimension of our profound humanity.

I have written the nine volume research series in an attempt to bring back the spirit of Dante's 'devotion' to looking more deeply into what shapes us and our world. His achievements became a stepping stone to the greatest renaissance of all times that began the greatest period of humanist development in the entire history of civilization. It is my hope that this still existing potential that Dante had one tapped into may be realized anew in our time. The principles that Dante had glimpsed so long ago are valid for all times according to the nature of principles. Consequently they are valid today. For this reason the great renaissance that we desperately need in our time has the potential of becoming realized. We are not looking for utopian dreams coming true, but for the truth of our humanity coming to light with a light "brighter than the sun" that had already been discovered several times before. We may yet realize that the potential for getting back to this light still exists.

Maybe Dante's greatest legacy is the cradle that holds the potential for our awakening towards an infinite future that remains forever within our reach to be claimed if we care to take the steps involved. Those steps comprise the critical choices that Dante had dealt with, which are now before us. But how will we choose? Will we explore the depth of our humanity and experience its freedom? Nobody can really answer that question. Nobody can see into the future. We can only look at our world as it is and explore the dimensions of the present civilization. What one sees in today's world is far from encouraging. In comparison with Dante's world we are in a far-more precarious state. Our economies are collapsing, choking with unemployment and poverty. Our world-financial system is disintegrating on the globalized platforms of imperial looting and slavery. And in the shadow we have war wrecking the world, now endless war, with atomic bombs evermore on the horizon that can eradicate civilization. And then we face the darkest and latest invention for the mass killing of human beings, the little-known dirty-uranium bomb that has already been pre-positioned by the millions, if not tens of millions, which could end human existence altogether.

During the years when the research series, **Discovering Infinity** was written to a large extend, the world was much brighter than it is today. Nevertheless it became evident at this time that a profound impetus was needed to power the transition of society out of its ever-deepening hell. It was seen as obviously impossible to eradicate terror with more terror, and war with more war, and the looting of society with evermore powerful looting by globalizing the process. It was recognized that we can only solve these problems asymmetrically by proceeding from a higher-level standpoint. Since the asymmetric countering of force, violence, and terror is to love, even to love universally, I began the huge task of writing a series of novels that is designed to explore the Principle of Universal Love. Over the years the work unfolded into the now 12-part series of novels, **The Lodging for the Rose.**

The series of novels, **The Lodging for the Rose** was preceded by two novels that serve somewhat like a preface for the series. The first of these novels, **Flight without Limits,** explores the hypothetical potential of being able to move instantly to wherever one wants to be in physical space. While we don't have that potential and probably never will, no such inherent limitation appears to exist in the mental realm. What inertia would hold us back in the mental realm, to prevent us from being where we want to be, or need to be? It appears that no real limit exists in the mental sphere where our humanity comes to light. Herein lies our future.

The second novel that preceded the series is the novel, **Brighter than the Sun.** It deals with the hell of a staged nuclear-war accident and the power of love that draws three families together by their individual struggles in countering this hell. In the unfolding story the Principle of Universal Love is gradually coming to light.

The reason why the platform of the novel was chosen to explore the Principle of Universal Love in parallel with the research series **Discovering Infinity,** reflects the nature of the response that is needed in our nuclear world to protect our existence and save our civilization that is rapidly collapsing into the shadow of terror, poverty, fascism, and imperial slavery and looting of the world. The Principle of Universal Love cannot be explored in a cold theoretical fashion to counter the darkness of these shadows. We would loose love farther on the theoretical platform, instead of facing its imperative in the world of our daily living where it should be our light.

The very concept of the Principle of Universal love needs to be uplifted in life by giving it a shape that is found in its practical development at the grassroots level of our social existence. Surely, Dante would have agreed that love needs to become an active universal impetus.

The 19th Century spiritual pioneers, Mary Baker Eddy, wrote the following about love as a principle that can only be understood in its universal manifestation rather than as a 'privatized thing.' She wrote: "LOVE - What a word! I am in awe before it. Over what worlds on worlds it hath range and is sovereign! the underived, the incomparable, the infinite All of good, the **alone** God, is Love... No word is more misconstrued; no sentiment less understood. The divine significance of Love is distorted into human qualities, which in their human abandon become jealousy and hate. Love is not something put upon a shelf, to be taken down on rare occasions with sugar-tongs and laid on a rose-leaf. I make strong demands on love, call for active witnesses to prove it, and noble sacrifices and grand achievements as its

results. Unless these appear, I cast aside the word as a sham and counterfeit, having no ring of the true metal. Love cannot be a mere abstraction, or goodness without activity and power." (Miscellaneous Writings, p.250)

Indeed love shouldn't be deemed something as small and rare like a gem that one picks up with "sugar tongues and puts on a rose leaf" for special occasions. It needs be the universal impetus, and it will be that when we can find it in the true face of the humanity of mankind that we all share and bring to light as human beings. It needs to unfold as an all-embracing, active expression, a light that enriches individual living. Only then can we expect to see our civilization unfolding on that higher level where fascism, slavery, war, looting, and poverty cannot exist, and the world is secure. Right now we are so far from this state that seems like but a dream, while the loss of civilization and the extinction of mankind loom in the foreground as a growing threat.

The series of novels, **The Lodging for the Rose** was written in parallel with the research series **Discovering Infinity** in order that it may enable us increasingly to see ourselves primarily as human beings - not divided by sex, marriage, wealth, power, but as a single humanity of human beings, individual in our living, but sharing a common universal human soul. In a sense, this is what Dante tried to convey in the **Commedia**. My series of novels is designed to take the Principle of Universal Love out of the theoretical sphere into the down-to-earth practical sphere towards a profound new renaissance in civilization. On this line the research series **Discovering Infinity** and the series of novels **The Lodging for the Rose** are designed to unfold in parallel.

Rolf A. F. Witzsche

# More works by the Author

Rolf A. F. Witzsche
http://www.rolf-witzsche.com

---

## List of novels - focused on universal love

http://books.rolf-witzsche.com

**Flight Without Limits**
(space travel science fiction)

**Brighter than the Sun**
(the nuclear fire)

**The Lodging for the Rose**
(spiritual science fiction - a series of novels)

Episode 1  - Discovering Love
Episode 2a - The Ice Age Challenge
Episode 2b - Roses at Dawn in an Ice Age World
Episode 3  - Winning Without Victory
Episode 4a - Seascapes and Sand
Episode 4b - The Flat Earth Society
Episode 5a - Glass Barriers
Episode 5b - Coffee Sex and Biscuits
Episode 6a - Endless Horizons
Episode 6b - Angels of Sex in Queensland
Episode 7  - Sword of Aquarius
Episode 8  - Lu Mountain

## Books of single stories from the novles

low cost books, for details see:
http://books.rolf-witzsche.com/stories/index.html

## Exploration books

http://books.rolf-witzsche.com

**The Lord of the Rings's Metaphors**
An exploration of the metphors in J.R.R. Tolkien's epic saga, The Lord of the Rings

**Small Research Books**
http://books.rolf-witzsche.com/stories/research/index.html

# Discovering Infinity

A research book series focused on scientific and spiritual development.
for details see:
http://science.rolf-witzsche.com

Volume ii (Introduction) - **Roots in Universal History**
Focus on Reality

Volume 1A - **The Disintegration of the World's Financial System**
Focus on Truth

Volume 1B - **Crimes Against Humanity**
Life Denied

Volume 2A - **Science and Spiritual Healing**
History as Truth

Volume 2B - **The Lord of the Rings' Metaphors**
The Future Determining the Present

Volume 3A
**Universal Divine Science: Spiritual Pedagogicals**
Structure for Discovery and Scientific Development

Volume 3B - **Science and Health with Key to the Scriptures in Divine Science** - The divine Principle of scientific mental healing

Volume 3C - **Bible Lessons in Divine Science - 1898**
The Scientific Process to Know the Truth

Volume 4 - **Light Piercing the Heart of Darkness**
The Demands of Truth

Volume 5 - **Scientific Government and Self-Government**
Platform for Freedom

Volume 6A - **The Infinite Nature of Man**
The Fourth Dimension of Spirit

Volume 6B - **Leadership**
 The Dimension of Leadership

**and other titles**